Are Blacks ✝ Spiritually Inferior To Whites?

RENAISSANCE PRODUCTIONS, INC.
601 Mantua Pike
Wenonah, NJ 08090
1-800-234-2338

Published by
RENAISSANCE PRODUCTIONS, INC.
601 Mantua Pike
Wenonah, NJ 08090
1-800-234-2338

© 1992 by Dr. Anthony T. Evans

ISBN 0-9625605-3-7

All scripture quotations are taken from the New American Standard version of the Holy Bible, © 1960, 1962, 1963, 1968, 1971, 1972, 1973, 1975, 1977 by the Lockman Foundation, unless otherwise noted in the text.

Printed in the United States of America

Contents

Acknowledgements

I want to express my deepest, heartfelt thanks to Rev. Richard Greene who assisted in compiling and arranging my research and helping me communicate my thoughts. His scholarly edge kept me asking the right questions. Thanks also goes to Mrs. Sylvia Vittatoe for the wonderfully gracious way in which she threaded through the mine field of my penmanship (or lack thereof) to provide a manuscript without spot or wrinkle. Both Rev. Greene and Mrs. Vittatoe reminded me of how inferior the inferiority myth really is.

Most of all, I thank God who taught me from His Word that I am indeed fearfully and wonderfully made.

Introduction

*O*ne of the most damaging and devastating myths perpetuated throughout American history is the supposed spiritual inferiority of Black people to White people. The destructive nature of accepting this myth as reality has had catastrophic consequences for the psyche of Black people, the world view of White people, and harmony among the races. Worst of all, it has hindered the church from being salt and light in the social landscape of America.

On one hand, this myth has kept the White church from sufficiently appreciating the massive contributions the Black church has made to a true understanding of biblical Christianity and from incorporating those contributions into its own ecclesiology. On the other hand, the myth has kept the Black community from fully understanding and appreciating our own heritage and using it as a foundation for addressing the cataclysmic crisis the African-American community now faces.

Another repercussion of the myth is that it has integrated itself into all aspects of our culture's psyche. Spiritual assessments carry great weight in a culture's ability to understand itself; therefore, when a culture allows a myth to dominate the way various groups within that culture relate to each other and to themselves, there will of necessity be great discontinuity on every level within that culture. Such has been, and still is, the case in America. This reality has led to our society's inability to understand itself--and what one does not understand, one cannot fix.

In this brief work, it is my desire to be one of many evangelical thinkers who help to dispel this myth which has not only impacted the racial groups of our country, but individuals as well. The effect of the myth on various groups has kept individuals hostage to the perspectives of their racial group, thus limiting personal development. Far too many Blacks are hindered from reaching our individual potential because of the Black group's demand that we remain in solidarity to the group's definitions and strategies for freedom, even though each individual may not share those same definitions or agree with the strategies. To avoid being viewed as an Oreo, an Uncle Tom, or a Benedict Arnold, an individual is sometimes tempted to retreat to the expectations of the group to satisfy the demands of the myth. While it is imperative that individuals not be so selfish as to be of little or no benefit to the legitimate aspirations of the group, it is equally true that the demands of the group must not impede, destroy, or dismantle individual responsibility, initiative, and goals.

Conversely, many Whites claim individual superiority because of the myth's doctrine of group superiority. Therefore, there is a great hesitancy on the part of Whites to sit at the feet of Blacks with the expectation of learning (as opposed to simply being entertained), since the myth has already defined the relationship as that of a superior to an inferior. The result is that the individual does not benefit because of the group's decision.

It is also my desire that this work will be one of many tools used by sincere Christians in putting the myth to rest and placing race relations in its proper perspective. However, it is my uncompromising contention that the only proper perspective is the divine perspective, for there are two answers to every question in life: God's answer and everybody else's, and everybody else is wrong!

Unless biblical Christians significantly enter the fray and take over the leadership for resolving the race crisis, we will be hopelessly deadlocked in a sea of relativity regarding this issue, resulting in restating more questions rather than providing permanent answers.

If the Bible is allowed to be the standard by which Blacks and Whites determine the truth, then freedom from this moral malaise will be the outcome; for as Jesus taught, the truth has a unique capacity of making people free. Only when we define ourselves and view our relationships in light of the absolute authority of Scripture can we begin to place salve on the open wounds that have kept America in perpetual racial agony. Even today, in racially torn America, there is a balm in Gilead.

Chapter 1
Understanding the Myth

Myths are traditions passed down over time in story form as a means of explaining or justifying events that are either lacking in scientific evidence or historical basis.

The study of myths, *mythology*, gives great insights into how societies answer questions about the nature of the world and the role of people in it. One very important element of myths is their ability to explain social systems, customs, and ways of life. Myths explain, to some degree, why people act the way they do.

Another fundamental element of myths is the strong religious tenets usually associated with them. It is usually this inclusion of the religious aspect that separates myths from folk tales and legends. Whereas folk tales and legends are developed and promulgated for entertainment and amusement, myths on the other hand are viewed as sacred and therefore true. For example, this is why Greek mythology centered on explaining good and evil through the creation of stories such as Pandora's Box and the development of its pantheon of gods.

The key point is that myths are powerful because they are believed. This results in myths becoming the standard and basis for the functioning of individuals, families, and society at large. Myths are like the development of a pearl in the mouth of an oyster. When a grain of sand gets caught in the oyster's shell it is continuously coated by the secretions of the oyster until a valuable pearl is formed. In the same way, the continuous secretions of societal standards justified by religious principles create a mythical pearl that is accepted as valuable by society.

Once these secretions harden and become embedded in the culture due to the solid acceptance of the major tenets of the myths by a majority of people and its leaders, their myths then become traditions that help define the culture. This is why Jesus had such a difficult time with the Pharisees of His day; their traditions had become so embedded in the fiber of Jewish life that getting the people to understand and accept the truth was no small task. Fighting myths can often label one as a revolutionary and even get you nailed to a cross.

When myths settle in and become traditions, they are then institutionalized, and the culture can hardly define itself without an intrinsic appeal to the myths that help create it and serve to maintain it. Education, politics, religion, economics, and every other arena of life are fair game for the myths' influence. Since myths tend to pervade all of society, there is no way to get away from them. Furthermore, myths tend to authenticate themselves; after all, everybody believes them. Once this happens, nothing short of a catastrophic upheaval can change or reverse them. The people of the USSR can give overwhelming testimony to what it takes to remove a myth that becomes an ideology which defines the existence of the whole society of which they are a part.

THE RISE OF THE INFERIORITY MYTH

One of the myths that has permeated American culture since its inception is the low level of spirituality of Black people and its resultant negative impact on Black culture. As European slave traders began invading, subjugating, and exporting Africans to the new world, their inability to understand and their failure to investigate this previously unknown people properly were the beginnings of the A-merican myth of the inferior nature of African people. Dr. William Banks summarizes the religious mentality behind slavery when he writes,

> The Portuguese and Spanish were the first Europeans to deal in the Black slave trade. Rationalizing that it was God's will to bring Black heathens into contact with Christianity, even if it meant a lifetime of enforced servitude, their ships carried slaves to labor in the Caribbean colonies as early as 1517. With the approval of their governments and the Roman Catholic church, the sellers of flesh maintained that "christianized" slaves were better off than free heathen.[1]

Since the slave trade was so extensive and so many of its promulgators claimed to be Christians, it needed to be legitimatized and justified. Of necessity, such justification had to find its foundation in religious principles if it was to be maintained and promoted with as little resistance as possible. This meant that the myth of inferiority not only had to be valid in the minds of the dominant culture that had created it, but it also had to be validated in the minds of those subjugated to it so that they would accept it as the nature of things in the real world. The theological contribution to the myth is expressed by C. Eric Lincoln when he argues,

There *is* and there *was* an American theology but
it is and it always has been a theology singularly
lacking in its ability to conceive of humanity
beyond the improbable boundaries of the White
race. It has always been a theology which per-
mitted and sometimes encouraged the sickness
of racism and which has on occasion grossly
distorted the faith through a calculated attempt
to fit the whole of reality into the narrow con-
fines of a doctrine of racial expediency and a
deep-seated commitment to a racial manifest
destiny.[2]

Thus, early in the exploration and development of the
New World, the capture of slaves was done in the name of
Christianizing the slaves. Since the "savages" needed "true
religion" to replace their paganism, it seemed naturally
justifiable to bring them to the New World with its strong
Christian, Puritan heritage for their own good. Never
mind, of course, that achieving that noble end would also
include the dismantling of African families, the raping of
African women, and orphaned African children as well as
many other attempts to destroy all continuity of African
culture. Sociologist Hank Allen writes,

They came into slavery with varying languages,
cultural traditions, rituals, and kinship net-
works. This, along with an unfamiliarity of
American geography, effectively prevented
slaves from developing the kind of complex social organization, technology, and mobilization
that would be necessary to alleviate their plight.
Moreover, to reinforce their brutal social and
psychological control, slave holders often
eliminated any bonds of kinship or culture by
dividing captured Africans into groups of mixed
tribal origins before selling them to plantation
owners.[3]

Since it was presumed that paganism was inherently part of the religion of the African and served as one of the primary reasons why he needed the new world, validation was needed from the Bible, the source book of the Christian religion, to authenticate the slave industry. The stage was now set for the infamous "curse of Ham" doctrine.[4] It was argued that since Ham was the father of Black people and since he and his descendants were cursed to be slaves because of his sin against Noah, then Africans and their descendants are destined to be servants, and should accept their status as slaves in fulfillment of biblical prophecy. This thinking became a major theological basis for American slavery.[5]

Now there existed a myth of inferiority with apparent biblical roots that supplied the captors with the fuel they needed to authenticate the validity of the myth. Not only that, but this provided the raw material necessary to convince the captured that to resist their assigned status as inferior was to resist the will of God. You now not only have a myth, but you have an authoritative myth rooted in theology. Twisted theology was now being employed to sustain a perverted sociology. This process is known as "sacralization," which is the development of theological and religious constructs designed to serve the interest of a particular ethnic or racial group.

Never mind, of course, that the Bible says that Canaan was cursed, not Ham. Thus, only one of Ham's four sons, not all four, was cursed. Therefore, all Black people everywhere could not be cursed. Never mind that the Bible placed limitations on curses for up to three or four generations (Exod. 20:5). Never mind that the curse on Canaan and his descendants finds its most obvious fulfillment in the ongoing defeat and subjugation of Canaan by Israel (Josh. 9:23; 1 Kings 9:20, 21).

Never mind that the other sons of Ham have continued to this day as national peoples in Cush (Ethiopia), Mizraim (Egypt), and Put (Libya). On the other hand, Canaan is the only son that has not continued to exist as a nation. Most important of all, curses based on disobedience are reversed when there is repentance and obedience (Exod. 20:6), which is certainly sufficient to negate the Christian endorsement of the American enslavement of Black Christians. Myths however, do not need facts; they simply need supporters.

Since, as in the case of most myths, the myth of inferiority needed as much religious and theological support as possible to make it stick, the New Testament was called upon to join the Old Testament in legitimizing the myth in the mind of both the captor and the captured. Biblical passages on slaves submitting to their masters (e.g., Eph. 6:5-8 and Col. 3:22) were called upon to contemporize the myth to the current sociopolitical and economic framework of the new world.

The Puritans were attempting to turn America into "The City on a Hill," that is, the manifestation of the prophesied kingdom of God on earth through the church. Slavery provided an economic base for implementing this theology, even among some of the theological and religious heroes of the New England colonial era.[6] The attempt was made to teach the slaves to accept their inferior status in as docile a manner as possible, for to do so was the will of God, but to fail to do so was to rebel against God and risk eternal punishment.[7]

With this comprehensive "biblical" strategy, the myth of inferiority took theological wings and soared into the sky of authenticity making the myth appear to be reality. Of course, the fact that Paul also told masters that they were to treat converted slaves as equal brothers in Christ (Philem. 1:15, 16), that slaves had the right to seek to change their status (1 Cor. 7:21), and that the authority of masters who claimed to be Christians was limited to that which was in keeping with the authority of God over them (Eph. 6:9) seemed insignificant. Never mind that dismantling the middle wall of partition means that barriers no longer exist between men's fellowship with God or each other (Eph. 2:14-16).

Also ignored was the biblical truth that to be members of the body of Christ means that preferences based on class, culture, or race are totally unacceptable to God and are candidates for His judgment (James 2:9-13). However, adding such additional biblical data to the myth of inferiority would demythologize the myth and tell the whole truth. Truth and myth do not usually mix very well.

THE PSYCHOLOGY OF THE INFERIORITY MYTH

The perpetuation of the inferiority myth is as much psychological as it is theological, because myths affect the way people think. This is true in the development of the myth of inferiority, which was forced into the psyche of the slave and often transmitted from one slave to the other slaves, developing what some have called "a plantation mentality." While this mentality has often historically and currently been successfully resisted, it nevertheless left its mark.

Historically, this was seen in the way many Blacks held their heads down when talking to Whites, perhaps wishing they were White themselves. The psychological damage was inflicted during slavery when corporal punishment was threatened for staring at a White woman; it was revisited in 1955 when Emmett Till was slain for allegedly speaking inappropriately to a White woman; and it reappeared in our contemporary time when Yusef Hawkins was slain for allegedly visiting an anglo female.

When a person is told either directly or subliminally that he is a "boy" even if he is the senior to the one making the designation, or when children are told they are "at risk" simply because of their skin color, thus decreasing their motivation to learn and validating many teachers' inclination that they are unable to learn,[8] the psychological damage can be overpowering. The myth of inferiority hits its mark again.

THE SOCIOLOGY OF THE INFERIORITY MYTH

The psychological aspects of the inferiority myth are reinforced by social structures that serve to undergird their impact. During slavery, the distinction between field slaves and house slaves, based on shades of lighter skin color granting greater privileges, helped to undergird the myth. Many laws were established that restricted equal access to public accommodations, such as restaurants, rest rooms, and transportation, making the myth appear socially acceptable since it was culturally and even legally promoted and enforced.

One of the most devastating social structures perpetuating the myth was the family structure itself, the most basic of all human institutions. Innocent White children were fed the myth of the innate superiority of their own race and, conversely, the ipso facto inferiority of the Black race. Such family transmission is extremely powerful in the development, reinforcement, and promulgation of the inferiority myth since the source for its authority is the very persons children admire and trust the most, namely, their parents.

The reason why the power of this myth has lasted so long is precisely because it bore the marks of parental endorsement; after all, "father knows best." When such parental authority is linked with the fear of the unknown and the misunderstood, it is natural that myths become authoritative and necessary for one's own survival.

Such was the case in American history. In order to legitimize their own self-definition as superior, Whites needed to also legitimize the status of others as inferior, resulting in caricatures regarding Black people in general. In particular, caricatures emphasized the Black male as oversexed, thus jeopardizing the welfare of the White female, and savage, jeopardizing the survival of the White male. Once such mythological representations were made, it was easy to justify laws to enforce the myth. For example, one such law was the infamous Dred Scott decision of 1857, which ruled that Black people were not legal persons, but rather property to be bought, sold, or killed at the whims of their masters. On the other side of the continuum was the promulgation of the inferiority myth within the Black family itself. Martin Luther King, Jr., said it best when he declared that no one can ride your back unless it is bent. The unfortunate reality is that the superiority myth with its powerful legal, social, educational, and religious support systems played well into the hands of those promoting the inferiority myth, even within the Black family itself; as a sad result, the backs of many in the Black community stayed bent. The myth made Blacks at times wish they were White, and it produced a path of self-destruction and character ridicule within Black culture. As a result, Black culture began to view large noses as a sign of ugliness and natural Black hair as nappy.

What is more, the church became another major contributor to the expansion of both sides of the myth. Hiding behind a hermeneutic based on cultural expedience rather than exegetical integrity, the White church endorsed the societally accepted status of itself as superior and Blacks as inferior. This endorsement came in the form of a deafening silence to the immorality of parishioners who bred slaves for profit and bred with them for pleasure. Furthermore, the myth was endorsed when Blacks were forced to sit in the rear of churches, if indeed they were allowed access at all. Also, it was endorsed when White denominations established schools for biblical learning that excluded Blacks who desired training in God's Word. This practice, which continued well into the second half of the twentieth century in evangelical Bible colleges, seminaries, and mission societies, accounts for the abysmally low numbers of African-Americans now preparing for ministry in those institutions today.

Such a view by the White church at large (even though there were many who rebelled against this hypocritical posture) reinforced a separation between the secular and sacred.[9] Even though this separation has been rejected by the Black church, it has continued to this day and hinders a comprehensive approach to cultural transformation. If the same value and energy given to protect the rights of the unborn fetus today had been given to protect the rights of the newborn slave because of his or her value before God, the church would have been responsible for setting the standard that would have determined the state of race relations in America.

With the rise of media influence in American culture also came the mass personification and reinforcement of the inferiority myth into every American home. Blacks were good enough to make America laugh at all types of buffoonery (e.g., Amos and Andy), reinforcing the general public's conception of the ineptness of Black people, even in the minds of other Blacks. Since such media representations did not spend too much time and energy exposing the strengths of Black culture, with the exception of athletics and entertainment, society at large was not able to see the comprehensive contributions these people of non-European descent have made to the greatness of America.

It was not until the Black revolution of the sixties that American society was able to see Black Americans corporately reject the inferiority myth, although attempts to do so have been made in varying degrees throughout Black history. With all of America watching, the shackles of second-class citizenship were categorically rejected, and the progressive push for inclusion was made. During this period, the media became a friend rather than a foe as the Black case for equality controlled the national debate and demonstrated graphically how debased the superiority myth had become. Laws began to change, opportunities began to come, enhancement programs were established, and massive amounts of funds were allocated and spent. All were designed to address the myth once and for all.

However, one problem still existed: myths do not die very easily.

THE CONTEMPORARY STATUS OF THE MYTH

American culture is still reeling from the effects of the inferiority myth. White Christians have lost out on the many benefits resident in the historical Black church. Although the Black church had its own distinctive and valuable appeal, it is presumed by the consensus of America that the brand of Christianity which comes through the broader evangelical community is the only significant vehicle of Christianity in America. Lincoln and Mamiya are correct when they state:

> The prevailing American sentiment has traditionally held that the mainline White churches constitute the only relevant spiritual pulse in the nation, and that whatever is outside this narrow ambit is of little if any significance to the American religious profile. This conventional wisdom is widely reflected in seminary curricula and denominational policies to the end that misperception is compounded, and the religious experience of some 30 to 35 million African-Americans is clouded in consequences.[10]

Generally, the tendency is to dismiss Black worship and church culture as something that is purely cultural and void of any true spiritual or theological fiber. The Black churchman is often viewed as a fanatic rather than someone who has a deep and authentic understanding and appreciation of God. The source of this misapprehension is that those who peer in from the outside have little or no access to the essence of Black church life and are the worse off because of it.

The Black community as a whole has always rejected the inferiority myth, although it has been severely wounded by it. Much of Black church history is made up of the process of rejecting the inferiority myth and attempting to set the record straight by protesting the superiority myth as well. This process was carried out by using the same authoritative source that was a basis for establishing the myth in the first place--the Bible. As the Black theologian J. Deotis Roberts asserts,

> This explains why the illiterate Black slave understood the Bible better than the learned White preacher or missionary who taught him. The Bible has a lot to say about justice, love, and mercy, about liberation from oppression, about deliverance from bondage, and about making life human. The privileged need definitions, rationalizations, logical conviction, and language clarity to understand liberation, justice, and mercy. A Black man reared in this society does not need a constitutional lawyer or a logic professor to explain "justice" or "injustice" to him. From early childhood the meanings of the words are apparent. Thus, when the Bible speaks of love, justice and mercy, its message goes right to the soul of the Black man.[11]

With the "Black Power" assault on the inferiority myth in the mid-1960s, recognition came that there was a need for a theology that explained, supported, and justified the new demythologizing process. The new Black theologians with a new Black theology began to articulate such a viewpoint.[12] Given the historical and vital place the Black church has had in the life and world view of Black people, it was recognized that a statement was needed from God validating "Black Power" and its response to the superiority myth.

However, in the twenty-five-plus years since the "Black Power" movement, many Black Americans find themselves still psychologically crippled with a low self-esteem derived from the inferiority myth which has had a devastating effect on the stability of the community. This is evident in the massive homicide rate of Black males between the ages of seventeen and twenty-five at the hands of other Blacks. It is evident again in the high teenage pregnancy rate, coupled with a generation of fathers who do not consider it their responsibility to care for the children they sire. It is further evident in the overcrowded prison population in which Blacks make up 50 percent of the inmate population, even though Black people represent little more than 12 percent of this country's population.

Most devastating in recent years is the promotion of the inferiority myth by the Black middle class against the Black under class. Many middle-class Blacks have accepted and even promoted a stereotypical understanding of "those people" by concluding that their brothers and sisters, whom they used to live next door to, are now beyond hope--a surprisingly similar conclusion that many Whites had about them.

The effect of the myth is also visibly demonstrated in the heavily dependent posture of the Black community in general, and the Black church in particular, on entitlement programs (welfare) which determine, to varying degrees, the community's right to survive. The independent Black church during slavery hewed out a community, culture, religious institution, and antislavery resistant movement with limited support from the broader culture. Unfortunately, the inferiority myth is seen in the institution's inability to do the same today, lifting the Black community out of its self-imposed plethora of destructive characteristics that seem to validate the inferiority myth's contemporary existence.

At this point, one might argue that the above-stated realities are not a result of the present existence of the inferiority myth's influence, but rather a result of the racism of the broader society. However, when a culture begins to destroy itself because of what outsiders are doing to it, something is terribly wrong with that culture. When the actions of those who illegitimately feel superior dictate the negative actions of others, then they must, of necessity, feel inferior to succumb to such dictation.

The great problem is that the inferiority myth is still with us, and like all myths, it carries with it great power and influence. In fact, it is persistent because Black people often, by our own actions, seem to legitimize the inferiority myth, which unfortunately is used by some to validate the superiority myth that spawned it. Noted professor Shelby Steele asserts this perspective on race when he writes, "The inferiority of the Black man always makes the White man superior; the evil myth of Whites makes Blacks good. This pattern means that both races have a hidden investment in racism and racial disharmony despite their good intentions to the contrary."[13]

The bottom line reality is that racial victimization, while a real problem, is not our ultimate problem. In fact, African-Americans must take a large share of the blame. However, to admit this would decrease our status as victim and delegitimize our racial demand upon others to fix what Black people must take primary responsibility for fixing ourselves. Just as "Whites gain superiority by not knowing Blacks; Blacks gain entitlement by not seeing their own responsibility for bettering themselves."[14]

Once a person realizes his unique position in divine history, however, he then begins to realize that no person or racial group has the final say regarding another person's or group's potential. This realization is by far the greatest need in Black America today, and unless it occurs, no amount of "raceholding" or political protest will reverse the situation African-Americans now face. As I have written elsewhere,

> Rather than spending so much time talking about how bad things are, we must begin to look for and operate out of our own strengths. Racism is real and evil. It must be resisted and ultimately defeated. But complaining about racism is only valid insofar as it reveals what we're up against. It is no more valid an excuse not to function properly as families than it would be for the

Dallas Cowboys to complain that they can't move forward because eleven other men keep getting in the way. The idea is to show how strong you are by going through, around, and over the opposition.[15]

To begin this process, we must demythologize the myth of inferiority so the mental fog that clouds the racial atmosphere can be removed. Both Black and White Christians will then be freed to relate to each other based on their mutual strength derived from the biblically based understanding of their heritage as it is rooted and grounded in the God "from whom every family in heaven and on earth derives its name" (Eph. 3:15).

NOTES—CHAPTER 1

[1]William Banks, *The Black Church in the U.S.*, p. 9.

[2]E. Franklin Frazier, *The Negro Church in America*, C. Eric Lincoln, *The Black Church Since Frazier*, p. 140.

[3]Hank Allen, "The Black Family: Its Unique Legacy, Current Challenges and Future Prospects," *The Black Family: Past, Present and Future*, p. 18.

[4]See the *Dictionary of Christianity in America*. "Curse of Ham," p. 333, for a summary of the argument and how it was used by the Christian church to justify slavery in America.

[5]Keil and Delitzsch take this view when they write, "The Phoenicians, along with the Carthaginians and the Egyptians, who all belonged to the family of Canaan, were subjected by the Japhetic Persians, Macedonians, and Romans; and the remainder of the Hamitic tribes either shared the same fate, or still sigh, like the negroes, for example, and other African tribes, beneath the yoke of the most crushing slavery. See *Commentary on the Old Testament*, vol. 1, p. 178, "The Pentateuch."

[6]Some of the noted New England leaders who endorsed this perspective of slavery were George Whitefield, John Davenport, Evera Styles, President of Yale, and Jonathan Edwards. See William W. Sweet, *The Story of Religion in America*, p. 170 and p. 285.

[7]See Charles V. Hamilton *The Black Church in America*, pp. 37-46 for a summary of how the slaves responded to this strategy.

[8]See Jawanza Kunjufu, *Countering the Conspiracy to Destroy Black Boys*, vols. I and II.

[9]J. Deotis Roberts summarizes "For Blacks there is no split between personal and social existence; the two are inseparable. Jesus as the liberator is also the Saviour. The social and the psychological dimensions of life and faith must be merged into one whole. Blacks know of no personal salvation that does not embrace the social concerns of life." *A Black Political Theology*, p. 137.

[10]C. Eric Lincoln and Lawrence H. Mamiya, *The Black Church in the African-American Experience*, p. XI.

[11]Ibid., p. 38.

[12]Black Theology has been defined by Joseph Johnson as "a systematic interpretation of the meaning and significance of the Christian Faith for the worshipping, witnessing, and proclaiming Black Christianity community. It seeks to analyze the condition of the Black man in the light of God's revelation in Jesus Christ." Joseph Johnson, "The Need for Black Christian Theology." *JITC* (Fall, 1974):19. C. Eric Lincoln adds, "Black Theology is a theology of Black liberation. It seeks to plumb the Black condition in the light of God's revelation in Jesus Christ, so that the Black community can see that the gospel is commensurate with the achievement of Black humanity." E. Franklin Frazier, *The Negro Church in America*, C. Eric Lincoln, *The Black Church Since Frazier*, p. 192.

[13]Shelby Steele, *The Content of Our Character*, p. 6.
[14]Ibid., p. 17.

[15]Anthony T. Evans, *Guiding Your Family in a Misguided World*, p. 168.

Chapter 2
The Depth of Our Biblical Heritage

*B*lack is in! The rise of the new "Afrocentrism" has provided a renewed awakening of Black self-consciousness and appreciation for Black achievement. The renewed interest in Egyptology and the study of African history and culture are highlighting again the unique role Black people have played in the development of the human race and world civilizations. This study is in no way limited to the sphere of Black scholarship, but anthropologists of all races are grappling with the increasing plausibility that the roots of human civilization are in Africa with Black people.[1] Rev. Walter McCray writes,

> The preponderance of contemporary evidence being gathered by archaeologists and ancient historians says that Africa (in Egypt's Nile Valley) was the origination of humanity and civilization. It was from here that humanity, an indigenous "Black" humanity, had its begin-

nings. The preponderance of archaeological and historical facts say that the roots of all people are in Africa!--Egypt, Africa.

> Whether one holds to the traditional view of a Mesopotamian origination of humanity, or to the more substantiated view of the origination of humanity in Africa, one point of harmony is certain: indigenous humanity and the originators of the civilizations in each of these areas were Black! They were Black in Egyptian Africa and they were Black in Asia's lower Mesopotamia! Either way one cuts it, the originators of civilization were a Black people.[2]

Such evidence includes the discoveries in the Tanzanian Canyon of Olduvai Gorge that reveal tool-making began in Africa and then spread to Europe. It includes the discoveries in the Nile Valley which demonstrate that people of Negroid African descent laid the foundation for much of its civilization and manufactured pottery before pottery was made in the world's oldest known city. Also confirming this thesis is the archaeological evidence that suggests African sailors explored the New World prior to Columbus. This evidence includes an extensive number of portraits of Negroes on clay, gold, and stones unearthed in pre-Columbian strata in Central and South America. There are also paintings by Negro people that date prior to 3000 B.C. Historian Lerone Bennett therefore concludes,

> Civilization started in the great river valleys of Africa and Asia, in the Fertile Crescent in the Near East and along the narrow ribbon of the Nile in Africa. In the Nile Valley that beginning was an African as well as an Asian achievement. Blacks, or people who would be considered Black today, were among the first people to use

tools, paint pictures, plant seeds and worship gods.3

There is, however, both a great strength and a great weakness in this new study. The obvious strength is in the very real self-authentication and self-appreciation that is realized as Blacks discover the depth of our historical achievements and contributions. It also touches the sheer need to clarify and correct the inaccuracies and deletions that have been taught by many who have bypassed the truth, by either the sins of omission or commission.

There is also a grave danger that must be avoided, however, particularly by Christians. If Black pride is to be legitimate and authentic, then we must circumvent the danger of failing to filter and critique Black achievement, history, and culture through the lens of Scripture. Greatness must be defined in terms of biblical criteria, not simple social theory. Black is only beautiful if it is biblical, just as White is only right when it agrees with Holy Writ.

It is crucial, then, that African-Americans prioritize the discovery of biblical heritage. Why? Because then we root our history and legitimacy in God rather than race or culture. While race and culture play a major role in linking any people with their past so they can proceed knowledgeably into the future, the history of one's race and culture cannot by itself serve as a sufficient starting point for authenticating one's self.

The questions then are: what is the biblical basis for Black heritage, how is that basis rooted in God, and what lessons do we learn from that knowledge?

The Bible and Ethnicity

The issue of ethnicity is a very important one throughout all of the Bible. Voluminous attention is given to the issues of race, culture, family trees, and geography as they relate to the identification of people groups. There is no such thing as cultural or racial neutrality. Every person belongs to some group. Even when groups intermingle, they either lean in their identification with one culture or the other, or they synthesize into a totally new group. Such was the case of the Samaritans, who were the mixed breed offspring of Jewish and Assyrian interbreeding. Understanding why it is important to bring the Bible to bear on ethnicity is crucial if people are going to relate properly to their roots.

First of all, because the Bible is the inerrant, infallible, authoritative Word of God, it is the only place we can go to receive a totally accurate and objective understanding of race. Whites and Blacks alike have both used and misused race for our own advantage. Both inside and outside our own cultures, we have allowed popular opinion, sociopolitical structures, cultural traditions, and personal preferences to "color" our views about ourselves and others.

Thus, Whites during slavery could overestimate themselves while Blacks could underestimate themselves. On the other hand, during the sixties revolution Black pride was sometimes taken to violent extremes. The Bible does not suffer from such human lopsidedness because it is divinely authored by a God who gives the "real deal" on who we are, what we are, and how we got to be this way. The Bible then is the best source for racial clarification.

Second, rooting racial history and culture in the Bible allows us to contradict those who would write off the Bible as a White man's book. When a person understands the glorious presence of African people in God's drama of the unfolding of human history in general and redemptive history in particular, it becomes clear that Scripture should be the primary source for legitimate Black pride. It is those who reject the Bible who stand on shaky racial ground, not those who accept it. Finding racial understanding in the Scripture allows us to take pride in who and what God has made us without feeling the need to become something other than what God created us to be.

Third, since race has played such a major role in social development and the functioning of American society, it behooves one to discover the divine response to attempts at victimization based on race. This was the problem Moses faced when his sister Miriam and brother Aaron rebelled against him for marrying a Cushite, an African woman (Num. 12). They allowed the color issue to become a social and political matter since it became the basis for challenging God-given leadership. Knowing that God rejected social rebellion based on racist attitudes is instructional for both White and Black people who allow racial decisions to determine social and political structures in America.

Fourth, a study of race rooted in the Bible links the pride and understanding of race with an eternal purpose. It expands our understanding of missiology. It is clear from Scripture that Black people are objects of God's love and grace. When it is seen that the very lineage of Jesus included Blacks and that the leadership of the first century church included Africans, then African-Americans can take pride in the fact that we are an integral part of God's redemptive agenda and have played a decisive role in disseminating that agenda to the rest of the world. People need to know the eternal dimensions of our history.[4]

The Bible, then, should be the primary source for legitimate racial pride, self-authentication, self-analysis, intracultural and cross-cultural critique, and determining a group's national purpose. The Bible alone can fulfill this function with honesty and integrity and should be the starting point for any group to find out who we are.

One of the ways by which individuals and groups are recognized is by our color. This is particularly true of the color Black. There is no biblical hesitancy in recognizing the value of color in defining either an individual or a people group. The biblical usage of color was unencumbered by the intrinsic negative distortions and reactions so easily associated with the use of color in contemporary American society. The color Black in the Bible is a useful tool of identification of people and races and, as such, should likewise be used today in a similar fashion.

Before I continue, let me preface the ensuing discussion by saying that actually there is only one race: "the human race." Yet the truth that varieties of peoples exist needs no supporting evidence. Although it is true that all humans stem from one root, Adam, it is important for us to look at the events and peoples of the past in order to determine who and what we are and should be today.

When discussing the issue of Blacks in the Bible, we must understand that the designation "Black" is a term of accommodation. By accommodation, I mean that we are using twentieth-century terminology generated by a twentieth-century mind set to discuss people who, in some cases, lived more than two millennia ago. Thus our distinctions are not necessarily their distinctions. Yet when we say "Black" in reference to those peoples of the past, we are on the one hand referring to physical traits African-Americans share with those ancient peoples, namely skin color; on the other hand we are referring to the genetic lineage of African-Americans and its affinity with peoples of the ancient Near East and Egypt.

Therefore, the answer to the question as to whether dark-complexioned people played a prominent role in biblical events is an emphatic "yes." Also, descendants of African peoples do, beyond a doubt, have an ancestral linkage to certain critical personages in biblical history.

One use of the color Black refers to actual skin tone of people from African or Hamitic descent. Such a descriptive use of color can be seen in the actual names of persons, people groups, and places, particularly in the Old Testament world. In fact, the descriptive use of names was very normative as a means of defining parental perspectives, hopes or circumstances concerning their children (e.g., as Rachel was dying in childbirth she called her son Ben-oni, "Son of my sorrow"--Gen. 35:18), or experiences related to certain locations (e.g., Marah, which means bitter, received its name because of the bitterness of the waters located there--Exod. 15:23).

Names also reflect the character or action of a person (e.g., Nabal was like his name, he was a "fool"--1 Sam. 25:25). Names are even changed when there is a need for a new description of a person, place, or relationship (e.g., Jacob is renamed Israel--Gen. 32:27ff; 35:10). Thus, biblical names are more akin to our contemporary use of nicknames when they are used to describe some characteristic of a person (e.g., red, describing redheads; or chubby for overweight people; or slim for slender people).

With regard to color designation, names are used to refer to the actual skin tone of dark-complexioned people. For example, Kedar means "to be dark,"[5] thus making the Kedarites a dark-skinned people (Gen. 25:13, Ps. 120:5). Phinehas means the Negro or Nubian, who were a dark-skinned people (Exod. 6:25; 1 Chron. 9:20). According to Exodus 6:25, Phinehas was the son of Eleazar and one of the daughters of Putiel, and his name literally means the Negro or Nubian. This is interesting indeed, because when Phinehas was born, Israel was already established as a separate commonwealth, although it was in transit. Therefore, within the commonwealth of Israel, at least some of the citizens were giving birth to children whose names characterized them as "Nubian" or "Negroes.

So then, the children of Israel must have been heterogeneous with respect to ethnicity. That is, there was probably a range of skin colors for those who considered themselves part of Israel. We must remember that the claim to the inheritance of Jacob was not a matter of skin color but instead a matter of lineage. The critical question was "Who was your father?" Remember that Manasseh and Ephraim were born to Joseph while he was in Egypt. Yet Jacob (Israel) made it very clear in Genesis 48:5 that Manasseh and Ephraim were to be treated as though they were Jacob's sons; therefore they were to receive an inheritance in the "Promised Land." Thus it is probable that the Nubian stock entered the line of Israel at this juncture.

Putiel's name perhaps provides us an important clue into understanding who his people were. The first three letters of Putiel's name appears to have a lexical/etymological link to Put, one of the sons of Ham.[6] Where the name Put is used in the Old Testament, it usually is named with African peoples (cf. Nah.3:9; Jer. 46:9; Ezek. 27:10, 30:5, 38:5). This would certainly explain how it was that Phinehas was born a Nubian in the midst of a Semitic congregation.

Furthermore, there were a total of seventy people from Jacob's family who entered Egypt (Gen. 46:27). Yet the Bible says that some 600,000 men alone came out of Egypt with Moses (Exod. 12:37). The total number involved in the Exodus, including women and children, is estimated at some two million-plus souls. There were probably other marriages to Egyptian women much like that of Joseph and Eleazar which would have produced offspring such as Phinehas.

In Jeremiah 43:7 reference is made to the place called Tahpanhes which means "Palace of the Negro." The name Ham means "hot" or "heat" and is taken by some to be an implicit association or reference to burnt or dark skin color especially since he was the progenitor of African peoples.[7]

Another example of color involved in naming conventions is the case of Simeon, called Niger (Acts 13:1). The Greek-English Lexicon of the New Testament comments on this epithet attached to Simeon in this manner, "Niger (dark-complexioned), surname of Simeon the prophet (Acts 13:1)."[8]

In the case of Moses' wife, Zipporah is twice identified as "Black" in light of her national relationship with the group of African people known as the Cushites (Num. 12:1). The Shulamite bride of King Solomon twice describes herself as Black (Song of Sol. 1:5, 6) ,referring to her own complexion. Of special note here is the spirit of legitimate pride associated with her recognition of her color, for she saw herself as Black and beautiful. We thus see from Scripture that to be Black and simultaneously beautiful is both possible and preferable.

Jeremiah likewise recognized people in terms of color when he raised the question, "Can the Ethiopian change his skin?" (Jer. 13:23). His point was Black skin color was as intrinsic and normative to the Ethiopian as was the unrighteousness embedded in the behavior of the nation Israel. It was a permanent characteristic.

Black Pride and the Bible

Since all humanity finds its origin in the three sons of Noah (Acts 17:26; Gen. 9:18, 19), this is an appropriate starting point for gaining a proper biblical basis for Black pride. Since all humanity stems from the same tree, it is idiotic for any group to claim ipso facto superiority. It was God's intention to reestablish the human race through the three sons of Noah; therefore, it must also be concluded that God legitimized all races over which each son stands as head and over which Noah presides as father. This is especially true since the Scripture says that God blessed Noah and his sons, and the command to repopulate the earth was comprehensive and equally applied to each (Gen. 9:1).

That these different sons represent more than personal family distinctions is evident by the fact that the ethnology of each son is associated with nations of peoples, as born out in the Table of Nations[9] recorded in Genesis 10. Black people then, like all other races, can take pride first in the fact that it was God's intention that we exist, survive, and function as nations of peoples.

One particularly instructional verse in this regard is 1 Chronicles 4:40 which indicates that Hamitic people living in Canaan were positive contributors to community life, productivity, and social well-being. Here, then, we have a biblical foundation for appropriately-placed Black pride.

Ham, Noah's son, had four sons: Cush, Mizraim, Put, and Canaan. Cush was the progenitor of the Ethiopian people validated by the fact that the names Cush and Ethiopia are used interchangeably in the Scriptures (Gen. 2:13; Gen. 10:6). Mizraim was the progenitor of the Egyptian people, who are understood in Scripture to have been a Hamitic people and thus African (Ps. 78:51; 105:23, 26, 27; 106:21, 22). Put was the progenitor of Libya, while Canaan was the progenitor of the Canaanites, one of the most idolatrous, problematic foes of God's chosen people, the Israelites.

The point is that whatever greatness is resident in the nations that find their roots in the sons of Ham, must find the heritage of that greatness in God. It is He who uniquely, sovereignly, and supernaturally authorized the racial differences that is the basis of those nations. Conversely, those aspects of historical culture that are against the character and revelation of God must be condemned as such since God as author of the races must be the standard by which any race should judge itself or be judged by others.

Of particular importance in this regard is the powerful Old Testament figure Nimrod, the descendant of Cush, who ruled in the land of Shinar (Gen. 10:8-10; 11:2). Nimrod eventually became the father of two of the greatest empires in the Bible, the Assyrian and Babylonian empires. His significance lies in the fact that he was the first great leader of a world civilization (Gen. 10:8, 9). The biographical data attributed to him stands head and shoulders above that given to anyone else, indicating how great he was among the descendants of Ham. He led all the people on earth and served as earth's protector. Nimrod's presence in history confirms the unique and early leadership role Black people played on the stage of world history.

However, Nimrod, in spite of all his glory, was catastrophically flawed for he led an international rebellion against the sovereign rule of God in history by seeking to establish a humanistically-led, one-world government to usurp His rule. Nimrod's leadership, as personally admirable as it might have been, led to one of the most graphic judgments of God in history. The point here is that racial pride and achievement must be tempered by theological analysis if it is going to be properly directed.

When one examines the biblical data, it becomes distinctively clear that Black people have an awesome heritage of which to be proud. This can be established on the veracity of Scripture. Black people should use the Bible and not society as the foundation by which we determine our value and not fall into the snare of allowing an inferior standard established by others, be they Black or White, to define and authenticate us.

Hamitic peoples were crucial to the program of God throughout Old Testament biblical history. Joseph's wife, an Ethiopian woman (Gen. 41:50-52), was the mother of Manasseh and Ephraim who later became leaders of Jewish tribes. It was the tribe of Ephraim which produced one of the greatest leaders Israel ever had, Moses' successor, Joshua (Num. 13:8; 1 Chron. 7:22-27), thus linking him in part with an African heritage. This Jewish-African linkage is very strong in Scripture. Amos the prophet said, "'Are you not as the sons of Ethiopia to Me, O sons of Israel?' declares the LORD" (Amos 9:7).

Jethro, Moses' father-in-law, from whom Moses received the greatest single piece of advice regarding national leadership, ministry organization, political strategy, and personal planning (Exod. 18:13-27) ever recorded, was also an Ethiopian from the tribe of Midian. Moses' wife, Zipporah, the daughter of Jethro, was Black, which also explains the furor caused by Moses' brother Aaron and sister Miriam (Num. 12). What apparently bothered them was not so much that Moses' new bride was dark-complexioned, since, as has been demonstrated, other Israelites were also dark-skinned; rather it was that she was Black and foreign. That is, her African ethnic origin was unacceptable in spite of the fact that she and her father had become Jewish proselytes. It is important to note here that God judged Miriam with the disease of leprosy for her rebellion against Moses "because of the Cushite woman whom he had married." Racism, whether based on skin color or ethnicity, has always been a terrible sin in the eyes of God and worthy of His severest judgment.

There is another very interesting observation to be made regarding Jethro. He is identified as "the priest of Midian" (Exod. 3:1). Since he was a priest, yet he was not a Levite and the Aaronic priesthood had not yet been established, the question is, "What kind of priesthood could this have been?" There is only one other priesthood within the framework of Scripture to which he could have either belonged or been similar to, namely, the priesthood of Melchizedek (Gen. 14:18). This is significant because Christ was a priest after the order of Melchizedek (Heb. 7:17). This means that the priest Jethro, who was of African descent, may have been indicative of pre-Aaronic priesthoods, such as that of Melchizedek, which foreshadowed the priestly role of both Christ and the church.

This, then, is another basis for recognizing the strategic role Africans played in the biblical saga that still continues today since all Christians everywhere, as part of the royal priesthood, are related to Jethro and his priesthood. Zephaniah the prophet was also a descendant of Cush (Zeph. 1:1), underscoring Black people as an integral part of God's revelatory process in both the proclamation and recording of divine revelation.

The Ethiopian eunuch, who probably was responsible for the beginning of the Coptic church in Africa, revealed the high degree of organizational and administrative responsibility that existed within the upper echelons of Ethiopian culture since he had responsibility for all the treasury of the nation (Acts 8:26-39). Candace or "the Kandake (NEB)" was the title given to the "queen of the Ethiopians" in Acts 8:27. According to the standard Greek lexical studies, the term "Candance" has been found inscripted upon Egyptian monuments and was used in Egypt to refer to the queen of the Ethiopians, corroborating the biblical account of Luke in Acts 8:27.[10] The word "Ethiopian" itself is of Greek origin. It literally means "burnt face."[11] The eunuch of Acts 8:27 had the honored position as treasurer in the court of Candance. The term eunuch does not necessarily require emasculation. It can simply refer to high military and political officials.[12]

Nevertheless this brief episode recorded by Luke is significant for two reasons. First of all, it acknowledges the existence of a kingdom of dark-skinned peoples contemporaneous to the major events of first century Christianity. Second, it records the entrée of Christianity into Africa. This account of Philip's encounter with the Ethiopian official verifies God's promise in Zechariah 3:9, 10: "For then I will give to the peoples purified lips, that all of them may call upon the name of the Lord, to serve Him shoulder to shoulder. From beyond the rivers of Ethiopia, My worshippers, My dispersed ones will bring My offerings."

By these verses one can easily observe the priority that God has to call to Himself peoples from the African continent, not into servitude and disdain as some incorrectly surmise, but into brotherhood with all men to serve Him "shoulder to shoulder."

Simon of Cyrene who helped Jesus bear His cross was of African descent since Cyrene is a country in North Africa (Matt. 27:32). The church at Antioch had two Black men as leaders within it by the names of Simeon and Lucius. Simeon is called Black (Niger) and Lucius was from Cyrene. These two Black men also assisted in the ordination and commissioning of the apostle Paul (Acts 13:1-3). Thus Black people were not only leaders in the culture of the New Testament era but in the church itself.

Deserving of special attention is the lineage of Christ who is the heart and soul of the Christian faith. Over and over again, the prophets prophesied that the Messiah would come through the seed of David. When the Davidic line is carefully examined, we are struck with the fact that Black people were included in the Messianic line. Solomon, David's son who continued the Messianic line, was born of a Hamitic woman named Bathsheba. The Table of Nations identifies Sheba in the line of Ham making it an African nation (Gen. 10:7). This may explain Solomon's features as being tanned of skin with bushy Black hair (Song of Sol. 5:10, 11). Of the other five women mentioned in Matthew's genealogy (Matt. 1:1-16) four are of Hamitic decent (Tamar, Rahab, Ruth, and Bathsheba).

The point here is not that Jesus was Black. To assert such, as some Black theologians and religious leaders do, is to fall into the exclusionistic perspective of many Whites who would make Jesus an Anglo-European, blue-eyed blond who had very little relevance to people of color. It would also fail to respect the distinct Jewish heritage of Christ. Rather, Jesus was mestizo--a person of mixed ancestry. Black people, like all other people, can find in Him a place of historical, cultural, and racial identity. As Savior of all mankind, He can relate on every level, to all people, in every situation. In Him, any person from any background can find comfort, understanding, direction, and affinity as long as He is revered as the Son of God, a designation that transcends every culture and race and one to which all nations of people must pay homage.

One might object at this point with the argument that there is little need for any recognition of the African presence in Christ, especially since it is argued that He transcends the cultural debate. However, since our culture has in varying degrees viewed Black as a curse, to show that Jesus had Black in His blood is to destroy that perception and its psychological legacy once and for all, since in Christ we find perfect man and sinless Savior. This knowledge frees Blacks from an inferiority complex while at the same time freeing Whites from the superiority myth. In Christ, we all have our heritage.

Even when we leave the pages of the New Testament era we run into African people of the faith who had a profound influence upon the expansion of Christianity. By far, the most scholarly and influential of all is Augustine, the Bishop of Hippo, which is located in North Africa, who is known as the father of theology. Augustine was an articulate speaker, writer, and thinker who argued for the recognition of the Bible as the authoritative, literal Word of God. Tertullian, one of the greatest of the early church apologists, was from North Africa, too. Both lived in North Africa during the period when it was dominated by dark-skinned people, a fact that not many Anglo-Christian thinkers are willing to concede.

It should be clearly evident from even a cursory under-standing of the Bible that many people of African descent have had a major role in the development and dissemination of the Christian faith. It is utterly unfortunate that if the biblical characters and church fathers were living in "Christian" America during the 1940s, they would have had to sit at the back of the bus, use separate restrooms, and be discriminated against in the realm of housing, education, and employment.

Far from being an uninformed, imbecilic people, our history is one of being a well-informed, progressive, pro-ductive, and influential race--so much so that we were at the very center of every aspect of God's activity in history. It is only because people have failed to tell the truth, the whole truth, and nothing but the truth that this reality is ignored. Without ever leaving the Bible, Black people have more than enough evidence to dispel the many variations of the myth regarding our inferiority, intrinsic ineptness, and lack of spirituality.

The key, however, is to take God's view and not man's view as the standard by which we judge ourselves and critique the judgment of others.

NOTES--CHAPTER 2

[1]See *Newsweek*, January 11, 1988 where a secular anthropologist and scientist grapple with the data indicating Adam and Eve were African.

[2]Walter McCray, *The Black Presence in the Bible*, p. 9.

[3] Lerone Bennett, *Before the Mayflower*, p. 5.

[4]McCray insists, "Black people need to understand all Black history, including that which is revealed in the Bible. If we are ignorant of our history and its heritage we will walk blindly into our future. And without keeping in our minds and hearts the spiritual and eternal dimensions of our history, our future

forebodes a hopelessness which many of us would rather not face.

From a Christian viewpoint it is important for Black people to understand their Biblical history. Understanding the Black presence within the Bible nurtures among Black people an affection for the Scripture and the things of the Lord. Far too many of our people reject the Bible because they don't understand that it speaks responsibly about them and to their experience. God is concerned about Black people. Furthermore, enough information pertaining to Black people and their experience is written in His Word to convince the honest searcher for truth that God is indeed concerned for the well-being, salvation and liberation of Black peoples throughout the world." Walter McCray, *The Black Presence in the Bible*, p. 31.

[5]The Hebrew lexicon by Brown, Driver and Briggs assigns the meaning to the root "KDR" Black-tented (see p. 871).

[6]The affinity between the names Put and Putiel can be observed in Brown, Driver and Briggs' *A Hebrew English Lexicon of the Old Testament* (Oxford University Press: London, 1968), p. 806.

[7]Ibid., p. 20. See also Professor Charles Copher's discussion on "The Black Presence in the Old Testament" in the work *Stony the Road We Trod* pp. 151, 152.

[8]For other early usages of Niger, see Bauer, Ardnt, Gingrich and Danker, *A Greek-English Lexicon of the New Testament and Other Early Christian Literature* (University of Chicago Press: Chicago and London, 1979), 539.

[9]For an exhaustive scholarly treatment of the meaning, significance, purpose, and interpretation of the Table of Nations for understanding and validating the Black presence in Scripture see both of Walter McCray's works, *The Black Presence in the Bible* and *The Table of Nations Gen. 10:1-32.*

[10]Bauer, Ardnt, Gingrich and Danker, *A Greek-English Lexicon of the New Testament and Other Early Christian Literature*, p. 402.

[11]Aithiops properly, burnt-face, i.e. Ethiopian, Negro. Liddel-Scott. *Greek-English Lexicon*, p. 37.

[12]Gerhard Kittel and Gerhard Friedrich, eds., trans. G. W. Bromiley, *Theological Dictionary of the New Testament*, vol. II, p. 766.

Chapter 3
The Glory of Our African Past

*A*t the heart and core of the inferiority myth is a mis-apprehension of Africa and its people. It is crucial that we understand the value of the African heritage as we survey the issues of spirituality and Blackness. Only through a proper appraisal of the past can we extrapolate correctly about the present and the future.

Much of the inferiority complex is perpetuated by a misunderstanding of the African influence on the slave's mind set. Contrary to popular belief, my conviction is that the African heritage of the slave prepared him well for both his spiritual and cultural encounter with the Bible. In other words, the tenets and theological structures of Christianity would not have been too complex for him or alien to him at all. In many cases, his own cultural and religious leanings would have bestowed upon him the faculty to theologize as efficiently as, and perhaps even more so than, his European counterpart.

To validate my point, it will be necessary to look at some key facets of African culture and religion without the impairment of western mythology. By "western mythology," I mean the corpus of beliefs and images which the western world embraces regarding Africans and peoples of African descent; views which are void of profundity and equity. Thus, in place of an in-depth view of African culture, the "west" supplies a superficial and degrading assessment of African culture.

It is this propensity on the part of Europe and its satellites to look upon non-European cultures uncritically that has effectively caused the western world to remain in the relational "dark ages," alienated from the rest of the world. In addition, since European colonialism has often brought with it the advent of Christianity into diverse places of the world, many non-Europeans assess Christianity through the merits of the ones bearing it. How unfortunate!

THE MISPERCEPTION OF AFRICA

Africa! At the sound of that word, images are conjured which profile Africa as a land untouched by the marvels of modernization. According to the typical, western-oriented mind set, Africa is a land of great wealth and plenitude in terms of raw materials, yet it has an extremely unsophisticated populace. The wealth of Africa is restricted to ivory, gold, oil, and coal. Noticeably absent from the list is the African himself. To be sure, at one time the African was viewed as a very valuable commodity; but that is just it, as a commodity, and not for his value as an image bearer nor for his intellectual prowess. Such a mind set spawns men like German Scholar Leo Frobenius who says,

> Before the introduction of a genuine faith and a higher standard of culture by the Arabs, the natives had no political organization, nor, strictly speaking, any religion. . . . Therefore, in examining the pre-Muhammedan condition of the negro races, [we must] confine ourselves to the

description of their crude fetishism, their brutal and often cannibalistic customs, their vulgar and repulsive idols. . . . None but the most primitive instincts determine the lives and conduct of the negroes, who lacked every kind of ethical inspiration.[1]

Frobenius would have done well to rehearse European history concurrent with and prior to the advent of Christianity. Neither Christianity nor Judaism is and never has been indigenous to Europe; rather, they are Middle Eastern in origin. Only via the prompting of the Holy Spirit and the military oppression of the Romans did Europe obtain the prize of Christianity. It was by no craving for virtue and ethical inspiration that Christianity surfaced in Europe or anywhere else for that matter. Furthermore, the trend toward fetishism (i.e., the worship of or the belief in objects understood as having magical powers, such as idols) is universal throughout humanity. Scripture verifies this universal trend toward idolatry in Romans 1:21-23.

> For even though they knew God, they did not honor Him as God, or give thanks; but they became futile in their speculations, and their foolish heart was darkened. Professing to be wise, they became fools, and exchanged the glory of the incorruptible God for an image in the form of corruptible man and of birds and four-footed animals and crawling creatures.

Even a cursory walk through the New Testament reveals many horridly distasteful practices among the peoples of the northern coast of the Mediterranean and the Greek-influenced area of Asia Minor to whom Paul wrote.

For example, in the Greek city of Corinth, one of the many deities that was worshipped was Aphrodite. Known as Venus to the Romans, this goddess was said to have had beauty which made the wise witless.[2] The worship of Aphrodite was centered around the temple erected in her honor. The liturgy involved sexual contact with the temple priestesses, that is, prostitutes. So enraptured were the Corinthians with this vile practice that Aristophanes (ca. 450-385 B.C.) coined the word *korinthiazomai* (which means to act like a Corinthian, i.e., commit fornication).[3]

In his commentary on Corinthians, Gordon Fee makes mention of the Asclepius room in the present museum in Corinth which is "mute evidence of this facet of city life."[4] It seems that on a large wall stood a number of clay *votives* [objects given in fulfillment of a vow or pledge] of human genitals that had been offered to the god for the healing of that part of the body, apparently ravaged by venereal disease.

Of course, we have always been taught that venereal disease came to Europe through Columbus' sailors who cohabited with the native women of the West Indies, which is another great western myth. In Corinth, however, we have evidence that venereal disease existed in Europe for at least 1,400 years before Columbus was even born! Nevertheless, if we find these practices common among Greeks, who were perceived to be the very pinnacle of civilization, then what practices may we presume the "barbarians," i.e., anyone in Europe who was not Greek, to have indulged in with an even greater flare for crudeness and licentiousness.

To reiterate, Christianity did not originate in Europe; it was Middle Eastern in its origin. Generally, the western world fails to acknowledge that the staple of western society, Christianity, is non-Western. For this reason, both Christians and non-Christians look to Christianity as the White man's religion, and because of this, there has been a call to Africans to return to their traditional belief.[5] Although I cannot in any way endorse a shift away from the faith to primal beliefs, I will acknowledge the need to examine our historical and cultural bearings to equip Black Evangelicalism better as a thorough theological enterprise.

I agree with the words of Timothy Bankole who said,

Putting Christ side by side with Buddha, Muhammad, or Confucius, I find a number of good and admirable attributes in the religions of these leaders, but Christ to me stands out as unique. This is one reason why in spite of the many despicable and un-Christian acts committed by some Europeans in the name of Christianity, I have abandoned neither Christianity nor the Church. In my personal life, I have found Christ to be all-sufficient, and if Christianity is practiced as Christ taught it, I have no doubt whatever that God's kingdom will come and his will for mankind accomplished even in our world and possibly in our time.[6]

In Search of a Link

When Europeans came to Africa, they did so with the idea that the African understood little, if anything, about God. They also had the idea that Africa had nothing to offer culturally or spiritually to the emerging and developing western civilization. As we will observe shortly, this notion was untrue in the past and is equally untrue in the present. It is precisely this ill-conceived notion that is at the core of the contemporary misunderstanding of Black people: our perspective, our methods, and our uniqueness. Furthermore, it is at the root of the misunderstanding of the Black church.

In order to understand any of these matters, it is necessary to have a rendezvous with African Traditional Religion. This rendezvous provides the cultural antecedent for the development of the Black church and its impact and influence in America.

First of all, a major issue of debate among Black historians and scholars is whether the slave adapted or lost his African religious heritage when he was brought to the American hemisphere. The debate historically has waged between Black historians, W. E. B. DuBois[7] and E. Franklin

Frazier.[8] DuBois argued that the Negro church was the only institution among Negroes that started in Africa and survived slavery. Contrary to DuBois, Frazier argued that it was impossible to establish any continuity between African religious practices and the Negro church in America. He argued that the crisis of slavery was too great to sustain African heritage. Moreover, the destruction of the native African languages marked the cessation of certain concepts which were incommunicable in English.

So then, the issue is whether aspects of African heritage were retained. If we did not keep anything from Africa, then the African-American experience is a totally new situation with no historical point of reference. However, if we did retain some aspects of our African heritage, it becomes a very important quest to know what was salvaged for the sake of determining continuity between the continents.

The prospect of discovering these links to African life was quite stimulating. It produced the sort of feeling I had when I watched the last episode of "Roots." Alex Haley had tracked his family tree all the way back to his clan, his tribe, and his history. It was exhilarating to watch the tears of excitement as they welled up in his eyes. One could not help but share Haley's joy of knowing, "I have roots. I have a history. I have a link!"

In recent years, the eminent Black religious scholar, Henry H. Mitchell, introduced a fine piece of work that establishes that DuBois is right and Frazier is wrong. He has established very concretely in his book, *Black Belief*, that, in essence, Black religion in America is a carry-over from African Traditional Religion. While not fully understood and appreciated today, much of what you see in contemporary Black religion is not only what you saw in slavery, but also, to a large degree, what you saw in Africa and, in fact, still see in Africa. Thus, to think of the Black church as a variant form of White missionary enterprise is fallacious. Rather, the essentials were already present; what Europeans provided was simply affixed to an already existent theological and social structure. The scenario is somewhat similar to that of Acts 17:23-31 where Paul, standing on the Areopagus, confronted the Athenian philosophers.

Men of Athens, I observe that you are very religious in all respects. For while I was passing through and examining the objects of your worship, I also found an altar with this inscription, 'TO AN UNKNOWN GOD.' What therefore you worship in ignorance, this I proclaim to you. The God who made the world and all things in it, since He is Lord of heaven and earth, does not dwell in temples made with hands; neither is He served by human hands, as though He needed anything, since He Himself gives to all life and breath and all things; and He made from one, every nation of mankind to live on all the face of the earth, having determined their appointed times, and the boundaries of their habitation, that they should seek God, if perhaps they might grope for Him and find Him, though He is not far from each one of us; for in Him we live and move and exist, as even some of your own poets have said, "For we also are His offspring." Being then the offspring of God, we ought not to think that the Divine Nature is like gold or silver or stone, an image formed by the art and thought of man. Therefore having overlooked the times of ignorance, God is now declaring to men that all everywhere should repent, because He has fixed a day in which He will judge the world in righteousness through a Man whom He has appointed, having furnished proof to all men by raising Him from the dead.

Notice that Paul acknowledges the history of the Greeks' recognition of God by saying in verse 28, ". . . even some of your own poets have said, 'For we also are His off-spring.'" This quote which Paul uses is from the Cretan poet Epimenides (ca. 600 B.C.). As the Apostle notes, the fact that we all stem from one seed certainly explains why certain patterns of belief in a Supreme Deity persist all over the globe. If a Greek could ascend to such grandiose thoughts of deity solely on the basis of general revelation, what would prevent the African from doing the same? The answer is nothing! All peoples grope for God. The difficulty is that our corrupt natures stifle our attempts to find an infinitely Holy God. The result is that mankind strains without efficacy through all sorts of ideological concoctions and images made by hand to reproduce the glory above.

Against this tendency to create a menagerie of pocket-sized deities made with hands, Paul, in verse 29, is firm in condemning such practices. But we would be culpable of exegetical myopia if we did not recognize that Paul insinuates that Greeks may have had a profound understanding of the things above; however, this understanding was aberrant in places and was not effective toward salvation.

When one reads Aristotle's *Metaphysics*, one would think that Aristotle was a Christian. Many of Aristotle's postulations seem as though they were extracted from the Psalms. Perhaps this is why the Catholic theologian St. Thomas Aquinas found him so intriguing. But to my knowledge, no one ever confessed his sins and accepted Christ through reading the works of Aristotle. Yet, it is clear in many respects that he was absolutely correct.

My point is that if we listen carefully to the sounds of African Traditional Religion, we might also find some profound reflections of biblical truth which might compel us to a greater appreciation for God, the Father of Jesus Christ, just as the African forefathers appreciated the Supreme Deity.

In order to understand and appreciate the depth of the slave's spiritual presuppositions, we must first grasp the process by which the African culture was transferred to America. When people transfer or are transferred from one locale to another, they take their culture with them. It is observable to both the professional anthropologist as well as the casual observer that when people relocate, they bring with them, in varying degrees, their influences, habits, perspectives, dress, religious inclinations, and a myriad of other aspects of their past.

One has only to visit almost any major city in America to find a China town, a little Italy, or a German town. Located in these specialized enclaves are specific things related to their particular histories and cultures. Any attempt to dismantle these subcultures is no small feat. Why? Because the very process of transplanting a people reinforces their need to retain as much of their culture as possible. They need to maintain a point of reference for themselves, as well as having a basis for critiquing the attempts of others to amalgamate them into the dominant culture. In the same way that parents raise children with a view on influencing their future life orientation and decision-making, cultures also raise children with the similar result that they have a distinct world view that is hard to shake.

Since it is obvious that even in amenable situations people attempt to maintain key elements of their own culture, it would be that much more of a necessity when the environment is antagonistic. Since slavery was a non-voluntary enterprise, the only hope the slave had available to keep from becoming like his captor and losing his own self-identity in the process was remembering and reinforcing his own cultural heritage. Such was the case as slaves resisted attempts to be deculturalized.

When people take their cultures with them to a new locale, it is the central elements of the culture that are the easiest to salvage. The centerpiece of the west African culture was God. All of life was interpreted in terms of the Divine. This explains why there was such a quick and easy gravitation towards Christianity and its comprehensive application in society. Since God was the African slave's reference point for all of life, He would be the first one to whom the slave would appeal, particularly in a time of crisis.

The reason this is so is because the world view of the Black American is the same as that of the captured African slave: God is central. This explains why the slave could not separate the sacred from the secular, personal sins from corporate sins, and religion from politics. It also explains why certain "low" religious practices of the slave had to be outlawed by the colonies. It was precisely because those practices survived the trek from Africa. This serves to validate the significant role of religion in African culture.

It is important to note here that "low" religious practices are a part of every religious environment. The Puritans conducted witch hunts to rid the colonies of witchcraft. Also, there were occultisms among the peoples of Mesopotamia and also in the worship of the mystery religions of the pre-Christian Hellenistic world. Therefore, African religion cannot be singled out as primitive savagery. As a matter of fact, there was no greater expression of "low" religion than was manifested by American slave masters where inhumanity was perpetuated in the name of God.

But just as the "low" side of African religion survived in the Americas, so also did the "high" side. Since the "high" side was complementary to the Christian God, it was integrated into Christianity and sustained by it.

One of the primary ways this cultural heritage was sustained is through the process of reinforcement. As the frequency of confrontation with one's culture increases, the greater the probability that the culture will be maintained. This was the scenario of the slaves. They were continuously in touch with their African past because they were continuously in touch with each other. Since new slaves were constantly brought from Africa to the plantations, they were bringing with them the African mind set which served to reinforce the African disposition, even in the absence of tribal and language similarities. The reality of segregation fostered cultural continuation.

The fact that such cultural transference actually took place and was not lost during the trek of the Middle Passage (nearly twenty million Negroes were made captive over the span of some 300 years [1517-1840]) is evident from a number of perspectives. As stated above, the fact that many African practices were banned by slave owners clearly demonstrated that those practices were in fact transferred. It is important to note that most of the practices that were banned had to do with African religion, such as voodoo practices, medicine men, and the rain dance.[9] The fact that this was true reiterates the central part religion played in African life.

Another indication of cultural transference was the adoptive system the slave community developed. Coming from a tribal/clan background, the slave was dependent upon his communal environment for security, serenity, and society. The slave recreated that environment in establishing what E. Franklin Frazier called "the invisible institution."[10] Christian clan meetings on the plantation became the new tribe. This is further verified when we observe the adoptive system of Black people in the migration from the south to the north. The plethora of "storefront" churches that arose was again the slaves' demand for a tribal/clan concept to provide them with a familiar surrounding in a hostile environment, with religion as the primary point of reference.

A final method of cultural transference was the rise of the new African priest, the Black preacher. The new Christianized leader of African people provided the cohesion and cultural reference point that kept the slaves in touch with the strengths of the past, the needs of the present, and the hopes for the future. Since African religion was handed down from one generation to the next by oral tradition, it would be natural for the African culture to continue to be transferred through that vehicle. The Black preacher became the channel for this process to persist. They were the new African point men in America who maintained the key elements of the African past.

Thus, it is now imperative that we examine the nature of African theological roots in order to validate the fact that the African background of the slave did indeed prepare him for the Christian faith. Through an analysis of African Traditional Religion, I will venture to show that the African slave's capacity to understand Christian doctrine was not inhibited, but rather assisted by his own cultural and religious predispositions. Furthermore, it will be shown that the liturgical basis for the slave church lay in these African traditions, supporting what DuBois suggested: that, indeed, much significant cultural continuity was maintained.

The Theological Link to Africa

The slave was not some backward, savage person who had no perception of the true God. He was already acclimated to God. Yet, as can be said of all cultures, the African recognized God through "His invisible attributes" (Rom. 1:19), but not unto salvation, for salvation is through Jesus Christ. That mankind has a general consciousness toward God is a tenet of Romans 1. Yet, it is the gospel that is the catalyst which affords all men salvation (Rom. 1:16, 17).

Since the slave trade primarily took its captives from west Africa, it is only natural that we begin our assessment of our African heritage from that area. We will look at African Traditional Religion through the lens of a prominent group of west African people known as the Yoruba. For centuries the Yoruba have lived in what is today western Nigeria. This examination of the Yoruba will provide us with a thorough and consistent view of the people of west Africa, from which Africa supplied America with forced labor.

The Yoruba did not have a systematic, propositional theology as such; rather, it was conveyed through the Odu, the vehicle of oral tradition. The Odu is a corpus of recitals used as a vouchsafe for the Yoruba doctrine and dogma.[11]

There are some 256 of these Odu; and to each of them are attached 1,680 stories and myths, referred to as pathways, roads, and courses.[12] Some have verses that are almost unintelligible. In these cases, it is believed that such sayings are profoundly deep and require special knowledge to interpret. In any case, to remember all of this data was a gargantuan chore for the village storyteller, a feat far in excess of remembering the entire King James Version of the Bible verbatim!

The question we face is, "How did the African perceive his God?" But first, we must consider the tone of our question. Historically, when people have asked this question the real gist of the interrogative was, "How is it that such simple people were able to grasp such a lofty proposition as the Christian's God?" The answer to this question is easy. The African's view of God was high, apart from Christianity.

As we observe the Yoruba form of African Traditional Religion, we see a very high view of the Supreme Deity known as Olòdúmarè. For the Yoruba, the name Olòdúmarè was magisterial and supreme beyond every other name. Does this sound familiar? Olòdúmarè was preeminent over all, whether on the earth or in the heavens. All paid homage to Him, including the pantheon of subdeities (also referred to as the divinities) who owed their existence and allegiance to Him. All acquiesced to His will without exception.[13]

For the Yoruba, theology was discourse about God, and it functioned within the matrix of life. Thoughts of Olòdúmarè were always synthesized with the *Sitz im Leben* (situation in life) of the Yoruba. Contrary to his European counterpart, theology was never an enterprise that was reduced to writing. The *modus operandi* of the Yoruba, as with other tribes in Africa, was oral recitation. However, an evaluation of the Odu will reveal startling affinities between the Yoruba concept of Olòdúmarè, the Supreme Deity, and Elohim/Yahweh (God) as He is revealed in the Bible. Below, we will compare the attributes of God as seen through the eyes of the Yoruba and God as the Bible presents Him.

One of the fundamental characteristics of the African's God was His goodness and justice. There was no thought of God ever being unfair. Given this fact, we might think that when the slave arrived in America he would have rejected his God because he was being enslaved in the name of God. Amazingly, rather than rejecting the high God, he tenaciously hung on to Him.

The only rational reason for doing so would be that, based on the slave's own understanding of God, he was sure that his master's interpretation of God was incorrect. In order for the slave to simultaneously love, serve, and worship the God of those who were enslaving, dehumanizing, and oppressing him, he must have had a view of God that exceeded that which was portrayed in the culture in which he now lived. This fact alone clearly demonstrates that African religion was not ignorant religion, but was socially-applied religion.

This leads me to a major conclusion regarding God's twofold, sovereign purpose for American slavery. On the one hand, slavery was allowed by God not so much to teach the ignorant slave savage the right way, but rather, as in the case of Cornelius (Acts 10:1-48), to acknowledge the slave's faith in the true high God by introducing him to Jesus Christ, the mediator who would replace all of the subdeities as the means of access to God. On the other hand, I believe that slavery was allowed as the means by which God would introduce the true meaning of His justice to a culture [i.e., American culture] which had neglected this aspect of His character.

Note the story of Joseph in Genesis 37-50. Joseph's final dispensation was that he was second in command of all Egypt. However, his ascension to this lofty post was tortuous. Yet, in his own assessment of his ordeal he informed his brothers of the truth. "As for you, you meant evil against me, but God meant it for good in order to bring about this present result, to preserve many people alive"

(Gen. 50:20). As Joseph endured havoc for the sake of an ultimate victory, so was the plight of the African slave. Such a view affirms not only what slaves received, but even more what America gained from this dreadful experience. If American society would submit to the justice of God the way slaves submitted to Jesus Christ, the power, presence, and impact of God in our culture would be beyond our wildest expectations.

There is a great deal of similarity between the attributes of God as He is revealed in Scripture and that Supreme Being known to the Yoruba as Olòdúmarè. First of all, Olòdúmarè was the creator. In the theogony or genealogy of the gods, all other deities were created by Olòdúmarè. All that exists owed its existence to Him. Thus, the heavens and the earth were products of the ingenuity and creativity of Olòdúmarè. In much the same sense, Genesis 1:1 opens with an all-inclusive categorical statement concerning the creativity of God (Elohim). Moses made use of a rhetorical device known as a *merism* ("the heavens and the earth") to demonstrate that Elohim has created everything from the top, which is heaven, to the bottom, which is the earth, and all things in between.

Similar to the Hebrew tendency to use different names for God to emphasize different aspects of His character, the Yoruba made use of this same convention. In His capacity as creator, Olòdúmarè was known as Eleda. Also, because Olòdúmarè was the origin and giver of life, he was called Elemi, "The Owner of the spirit" or "The Owner of life."

Not only was Olòdúmarè considered to be the creator, but he was "the king of the universe" as well. He was over men as well as the other deities which he created. In the Book of Psalms, Psalms 47, 93, and 96-99 are all dedicated to the kingship of Yahweh. For example, Psalm 93:1, 2 reads "The LORD (Yahweh) reigns, He is clothed with majesty; the LORD has clothed and girded Himself with strength; indeed, the world is firmly established, it will not be moved. Thy throne is established from of old, Thou art from everlasting." In much the same way that the Israelites used these "enthronement" psalms to acknowledge the majesty and authority of Yahweh, the Yoruba employed various chants reflecting the same ideas about Olòdúmarè. To the Yoruba, Olòdúmarè was also omnipotent. He was the most powerful being in the entire universe. He was able to do all things. The Yoruba would have had no difficulty at all grasping the affirmations in Genesis 18:14, Jeremiah 32:17, Matthew 19:26, and Luke 1:37, all of which affirmed that "there is nothing that God cannot do." The Yoruba thought also that things were possible only when and because they were ordered by Olòdúmarè. Isaiah 46:9, 10 affirms this same sentiment, namely, that God orders all things after the counsel of His own will (see also Eph. 1:11).

Olòdúmarè was all-wise, all-knowing and all-seeing. He and he alone was impeccable and omniscient. The sub-deities might err, but not the Supreme Deity. An analogy with the Scripture of the Old Testament can be found in Psalm 139. Yahweh is portrayed as the One who sees and knows all. Nothing is hidden from His sight. Olòdúmarè was called Olorun when referring to His wisdom. A line in one of the songs reads *Kil'e nse ni bekulu t' oju olorun o to?*--"Whatever do you do in concealment that Olorun's eyes do not reach?"[14]

According to E. Bolaji Idowu, in the Yoruba conception of "The Last Things", "Olòdúmarè is the final Disposer of all things. He is the Judge. He controls man's destiny, and each will receive from Him as he deserves."[15] This motif, that God is the judge of the world, may be seen in several places in Scripture. In Genesis 18:25, Abraham says that God is "the Judge of all the earth." Psalm 7:11 states that God is a "righteous judge." Romans 2:16 reports that one day God will judge men's secrets. 1 Peter 4:5 says that He will "judge the living and the dead."

So strong was the appreciation for the sovereignty and justice of Olòdúmarè that the Yoruba typically avoided seeking revenge for crimes perpetrated against them. They trusted that Olòdúmarè would render proper recompense for evil. Wickedness would not receive any impunity before Olòdúmarè. "Vengeance is Mine, I will repay" would be totally in line with the Yoruba concept of justice and sovereignty. In the mind set of the African and of his progeny, the phrase Fortune Imperatrix Mundi [Fate, the ruler of the world] never applied, for God was supreme, He ruled, and all would answer to Him, without exception. Far too often, we in the western world tend to think that morality and impartiality are western Christian concepts. Much to the chagrin of the western world, it is not. God's law is universal. The morality that men do have is there because men are image-bearers. We need not try to superimpose our cultural values upon people of diverse places, all the while assuming that our cultural values are uniquely "Christian." God has left a witness of Himself in many places. Therefore, we should not only do exegesis in the Scripture, but also in the world in which we live.

In America, we suffer from a "Rambo" complex. We feel compelled to pay back "evil for evil." If we do not pay back, we feel emasculated and spineless. It is much harder to let our need for revenge go, knowing that God will always deal the last hand. Whereas this concept of allowing God to judge is difficult for Americans, it has always been a way of life for the Yoruba. How interesting. The people without the Bible are sometimes more biblical than those who have it!

Immortality, also an attribute of "the Deity," was foremost in the Yoruba concept of the Supreme Deity. This aspect was emphasized often and in many ways. One of the Yoruba songs states, "One never hears of the death of Olòdúmarè." From excerpts of other Odu recitals, we find that Olòdúmarè was known as "The Mighty, Immovable Rock that never dies." As Idowu comments, "In a sense, this is a comfort and encouragement to the worshipping soul. It is necessary to know that the Deity is alive forevermore, that He is unchanging in the midst of all the changes and decay which have been the constant experience of man, if religion and life are to have any ultimate meaning."[16] As in Christianity, concomitant with the concept of immortality is that of immutability. As stated by A. A. Hodge,

> By his immutability we mean that it follows from the infinite perfection of God; that he can not be changed by any thing from without himself; and that he will not change from any principle within himself. That as to his essence, his will, and his states of existence, he is the same from eternity to eternity. Thus he is absolutely immutable in himself. He is also immutable relatively to the creature, insomuch as his knowledge, purpose, and truth, as these are conceived by us and are revealed to us, can know neither variableness nor shadow of turning--James 1:17.[17]

Although the Yoruba used a different genre to express his theology, it possessed every bit of the precision and comprehensiveness that Hodge displays through his own keen expression. In the place of extended discourse in propositional form, the Yoruba supplied terse and pithy metaphors which defined his perception and expression of the greatness of Olòdúmarè.

Olòdúmarè was also considered holy. But here, we must proceed with caution. For as Idowu warns,

> What can be gathered from our sources about the holiness of Olòdúmarè is only by inference. The idea of holiness in the sense of "separateness" is already implied in the emphasized uniqueness of his essential qualities. He is transcendent; so transcendent is He that the fact of His immanence has received little emphasis except, of course, in the implicit understanding that He is there all the time, in control of the whole course of nature, and available to man whenever or wherever he is called upon. But the clear idea

of "The Holy" in the sense of the active, swift, consuming "numinous" is lacking in the Yoruba conception of the Deity Himself.[18]

It is clear that the Yoruba saw Olòdúmarè as pure. In the Odu recitals, the language used to express this innate quality of Olòdúmarè is surprisingly close to that of the Bible. For example, Olòdúmarè was referred to as "The Pure King," "The One clothed in White Robes, Who dwells above." But the concept of a consuming holiness, one that is beyond measure so that it remains veiled from men, was not resident in the religion of the Yoruba. For Romans 1:21 explains, "For even though they knew God, they did not honor Him as God."

It is insufficient for men to simply acknowledge the existence of God. Men do this simply on the basis of general revelation. But since humans are in a fallen state, they do not properly comprehend God as He truly is. For this reason, we are to identify God through Jesus Christ, in order that all may know the kind of God to which we refer, namely, the God who requires holiness and righteousness above all things. It is Jesus Christ and Him alone who gives us a full disclosure as to what is meant by the holiness of God. The Apostle John says, "No man has seen God at any time; the only begotten God [Jesus] who is in the bosom of the Father, He has explained Him" (John 1:18). The word in Greek is *exegeomai* which means "explain, interpret."[19] Thus, the Father has been explained through Jesus Christ.

Although holiness for the Yoruba did not carry an exact connotation as the concept of holiness in Christianity, because of their disposition for allegiance to God and their utter dependence on Him for everyday life, it would have been no problem at all for the Yoruba to add this facet of worship to their already high view of God.

There is another significant theological concept that I must mention before I proceed. This is the concept of sacrifice. The institution of the sacrifice was an integral element of the life of the Yoruba. It was through the sacrificial system that one found approval before Olòdúmarè and appeased the divinities. The basic idea was "seek favor from the gods" and "drive off the evil spirits."

Offerings were never offered directly to Olòdúmarè, but through several mediators, some human (the priests) and some spiritual (the divinities). In Christianity, there is only one mediator between man and God (1 Tim. 2:5). It is Jesus alone who is our advocate before the throne. In their roles as mediators, the divinities of the Yoruba bore the supplications of the people before the presence of the Supreme Deity. This was cosmic protocol. No one man could come near to Olòdúmarè. This was not only done in practice but moreover it was considered impossible.

Because the Yoruba had such a transcendent view of God, it was difficult for them to accept that the God of Christianity wanted to be near to them. Their concern was, "How could a God so wonderful come close to ones such as us?" So then, the difficulty with the "closeness of God" theme in the Bible was not born out of ignorance, but out of reverence. But as for the basic concept of mediation itself, the Yoruba had no problem, although certainly their views on how many mediators there were required a significant alteration.

I feel it worthy to mention that the Yoruba did at one time practice human sacrifice. This is no longer practiced today. Peace between the tribes and the advent of the British extinguished this practice. Sometimes human sacrifices were offered in order that they might be advocates before the divinities. Thus, the Africans would have had no problem whatsoever comprehending the role of Christ as advocate before the throne of God.[20]

Human sacrifice was only done in dire circumstances, namely when the livelihood of the community was at stake. Usually, the victim was someone who had been captured in a war. Very seldom was the victim a member of the village. As previously mentioned, a member of the tribe was slated for sacrifice to be an emissary for the community before the gods. Here, we see an advocate motif.

It is clear from the witness of Scripture that human sacrifice is an abominable practice, one that the Bible condemns. It was common in the Middle East during the days of the Old Testament. The Old Testament refers to the sacrifices done to Molech, the god of the Ammonites. This was a detestable practice before God and He made this known to Israel in Leviticus 20:1, 2: "The Lord spoke to Moses, saying, 'You shall also say to the sons of Israel, "Any man from the sons of Israel or from the aliens sojourning in Israel, who gives any of his offspring to Molech, shall surely be put to death."'" Thus, human sacrifice was not to be a convention of the religious life of Israel. All sacrifice was to be done after the prescription of God's edicts concerning sacrifice in Leviticus. This meant that there would be a categorical moratorium on human sacrifice of any kind!

As we can clearly see, the Yoruba had an enormously deep appreciation for God and His ways. In fact, the appreciation was so profound that their belief system mirrored that of Christianity in many respects. Therefore, the leap from African Traditional Religion to Christianity would not have been a quantum leap, but rather a simple transition.

The discussion of similarities and disparities could go on ad infinitum, but I propose that it is sufficient to state that the African Traditional Religion of the Yoruba would have prepared them well for their entree into Christianity. Also, from the heritage bestowed upon them by African Traditional Religion, we see three major repercussions that echoed into the African-American church: (1) the tendency and focus on oral communication, (2) the tendency toward orthodoxy and a high view of God, and (3) a strong connection between theology and life. These three areas are at the heart of a comprehensive view of Christianity.

NOTES--CHAPTER 3

[1]Leo Frobenius, *The Voice of Africa*, (London: Oxford University Press, 1913), l:xiiif.O.

[2]Edith Hamilton, *Mythology*, (Mentor: New York and Scarborough, Ontario, 1969), pp. 32, 33.

[3]Corinth, *The International Standard Bible Encyclopedia*, vol. 1, (Eerdmans: Grand Rapids, 1979), p. 773.

[4]Gordon Fee, *The First Epistle to the Corinthians*, (Eerdmans: Grand Rapids, 1987), p. 2.

[5]C. Olowola, "The Concept of Sacrifice in Yoruba Religion," DTS Thesis, August 1976, p. 3.

[6]Quoted in Olowola's thesis is Timothy Bankole's work, *Missionary Shepherds and African Sheep*, (Ibadan: Daystar Press, 1971), p. 6.

[7]W. E. B. DuBois, *The Negro*, (New York: Oxford University Press, 1970), pp. 113, 114.

[8]Franklin's arguments are found in his book. E. Franklin Frazier, *The Negro Church in America*, (New York: Schocken Books, 1963), pp. 9-19.

[9]The rain dance was where the slaves moved in a circle counterclockwise as they danced. This kind of dancing is still common in Africa today.

[10]E. Franklin Frazier coined this phrase, "the invisible institution" to refer to the informal development of Black religion prior to it developing official organization structure.

[11]E. Bolaji Idowu, *Olòdúmarè God in Yoruba Belief*, (Longmans: London, 1962), p. 7.

[12]Ibid., pp. 38-47.

[13]Ibid.

[14]Ibid., p. 41.

[15]Ibid.

[16]Ibid., pp. 42, 43.

[17]A. A. Hodge, *Outlines in Theology*, (Banner of Truth: Carlisle, Pennsylvania), p. 143.

[18]Idowu, *Olòdúmarè God in Yoruba Belief*, pp. 46, 47.

[19]Bauer, Ardnt, Gingrich and Danker, *A Greek-English Lexicon of the New Testament and Other Early Christian Literature*, (University of Chicago Press: Chicago and London, 1979), p. 275.

[20]See Olowola, p. 119.

Chapter 4

The Greatness of the Black Church

*T*he historical Black church is the result of the fusion of the best of African culture and the Christian faith. Such a fusion gave rise to what was probably one of the clearest expressions of New Testament Christianity America has ever seen. This is so because of the natural way the slave community adapted to Christianity, coupled with the similarities that existed between the experience of the Jews in both the Old and New Testaments, and their own social situation. Such a link made untenable any separation of church and state, for one could not speak of life apart from theology.

When the development of the Black slave church is analyzed from the standpoint of the Black community itself as opposed to the broader culture, it becomes extraordinarily clear that it developed out of the strengths of the Black community, not out of its weaknesses. This development reflects the depth of the slave's theistic orientation to life and this people's unique adaptability in placing God in any situation and finding in Him the solution to their life problems.

When we examine the New Testament definition of the church and juxtapose it next to the functioning of the historical Black church, it becomes clear that the two institutions were very similar. As such, these two institutions are in a unique position to teach both the Black and White churches of today what true biblical Christianity looks like when it operates in a church that truly makes God the center of its existence.

THE BIRTH OF THE BLACK CHURCH

It is unfortunate that many people see the origin of the Black church as little more than a religion aside from mainstream biblical Christianity. However, when one comes to understand and appreciate fully the conditions and circumstances that came together to give rise to this unique institution, it becomes clear early on that the origin of the Black church reveals that its makeup consisted of men and women of tremendous depth, intellect, wisdom, and pride, who were willing to submit all of these virtues to the work of a sovereign God.

The birth of the Black church was the result of a confluence of five strategic factors. First of all, the reality of slavery forced the slave to look within himself for meaning. Upon their arrival in America, the slaves found themselves in a most precarious position, that is, there existed no freedom, no meaning, no hope, and no help. Where then were they to turn to find these desperately needed facets of life? Well, they looked at the only place available, which was within themselves, their history, their culture, and their religious heritage. There they saw the most significant aspect of their past life in Africa: God!

"It is probable that the African wholistic view of God was such an important affirmation of Black selfhood that its sense of 'God all in me' was among the most important resources for survival in the unprecedented dehumanization of American slavery."[1] They had to look to that God whom they celebrated in West Africa for His provision of meaning, hope, and freedom, to give them that same definition of existence in their new hostile environment. Immediately, the slaves had the one thing that could keep them"keeping on" despite the social reality of their plight; they had their God.

Such a realization of the necessity for faith in the centrality of God resulted in the prioritization of the spiritual dimensions of life. The slaves' mind was thus already preconditioned for the key role the Black church would play in their lives. This intuitive theistic mind set also reveals the depth of the divine consciousness within them.

Second, White organizations, such as The Anglican Society for the Propagation of the Gospel, and movements such as the first Great Awakening, began evangelizing the slaves.[2] What is critical to understand here is that this evangelization process occurred without addressing the oppressed condition in which these African transplants had been incarcerated. In 1667, for example, the Virginia Legislature agreed that baptism did not alter the state of the slave. Such laws then allowed Blacks to be evangelized without ever having to address their social-political plight.

With the influence of the first Great Awakening, Christianity was brought to the level of the common man. This made the African feel comfortable with the appeal of Christianity to the common man, especially since the slave was as common a man as you could find. Many of these revivals and crusade meetings were full of emotion, shouting, dancing, and other verbal expressions. This reminded the slaves of their own worship experiences and helped to make Christianity palatable to them.

Third, slaves began integrating their African beliefs with the new revelations they were hearing concerning the Christian faith. This integration process revealed the intellectual capacity of the slaves, for when they heard the message of the gospel, they heard more than just personal forgiveness of sin. They heard the voice of hope. The Christian message spoke of the hope of heaven where earthly trials would be no more and where there existed the freedom from all the injustices they were experiencing. They heard about a God who loved them and suffered for them that they might experience eternal freedom. Given the cry for freedom and given the magnitude of God's suffering love with which the slave could easily identify, the stage was set for finding that freedom in Christianity.

However, in Christianity the slaves also found a message of liberation from the oppressive historical condition of slavery. The Christian message was latched onto as their impetus for survival, self-authentication, and historical freedom. The integration of the eternal and the temporal was evidenced in the worship services of the slaves. They would dress up for their worship services and mimic some of their African rituals in this new Christian environment. Secret worship meetings were held if the master did not officially allow them to gather together because of his view against the Christianization of the slave or because of his fear of possible insurrection.

It was at these secret meetings that codes were developed enabling the slaves to communicate with each other. These codes were communicated in slave songs,[3] which was a major means of communication in African Traditional Religion. For example, one of the slaves would start singing "Steal away, steal away to Jesus." What this meant was that when the sun went down there was going to be a church meeting in the swamp so steal away to the service.

Songs, then, were not just for personal pacification in their circumstances. They were also a mechanism for community planning, again revealing both the strong intellectual prowess of the slaves as well as their religious commitment to the high God in that they were willing to risk punishment in order to maintain the priority of worship.

Swamps and forests became the early sanctuaries for slave worship services. On the following morning in the field, the slaves would break out with a song, "I couldn't hear nobody praying," which meant that the master could not hear the worship service going on and thus the secret nature of the worship had been accomplished. The early African slave church, then, was made up of a brilliant cadre of men and women who had to code their communicative expertise in the natural movement of their lives, with God at the center.

Fourth, the Bible became the first book to which the slaves were exposed. This exposure provided the slaves with a powerful understanding of God's activity on behalf of His people in history. The nature of slavery was such that those parts of the Bible demonstrating deliverance were emphasized.

As the Black community began to be exposed to the Bible and the person of Jesus Christ, it became acutely aware that the Bible was deeply concerned with the subject of freedom in history as well as eternity. As the Bible was examined by the few who were able to read during the early days of the Black church, the more they became attuned to the fact that God had in the past worked with another group of people called the Israelites who were, like the Africans, under bondage in a foreign land.

As the story unfolded, it became clear that God was not only concerned about their condition because of His love for them, but he also desired to free them from that condition of bondage. This story became the basis for the temporal hope of the slaves. The slaves concluded that if God could save Israel from Egyptian oppression, He could certainly save Black people oppressed in America. Thus the story of Israel's deliverance was a story which was easy for the slaves to transpose to their own existential experience.

This is especially true since there was no division or distinction between the Black church and the Black community, intensifying the parallel between Israel and Black Americans as covenant communities. It became clear with this story that God was on the side of the slaves and against the oppression of their masters. Here again, the slaves demonstrated a much superior understanding of the nature of God as it related to history. Israel's story became the Black community's "story."[4]

The fifth and final factor that led to the development of the Black church was the rise of the Black preacher who would provide the link between Africa and America. We shall look at this unique leader in more detail in a later chapter.

THE BLACK CHURCH, CHRIST, AND BIBLICAL LIBERATION

The Black church did not arrive at its Christology through academic study, but rather through the religious experience it was forced to have in the context of slavery. The social context of Black religion shaped its views of Jesus. This is not to say that academic information was not available to the Black church, but it is to say that the conditions under which that information was received greatly helped to shape how the Black church internalized and responded to it. The fact that the Black church came into existence in the context of slavery meant that it had questions forced upon it that needed answering. These questions reflected the journey the slaves made in seeing them answered. The journey was one leading from slavery to freedom.

For example, the slaves sang,

> I want Jesus to walk with me,
> I want Jesus to walk with me,
> All along my pilgrim's journey
> I want Jesus to walk with me.
>
> In my trials, walk with me,
> In my trials, walk with me,
> When the shades of life are falling,
> Lord, I want Jesus to walk with me.

He walked with my mother, He'll walk with me.
He walked with my mother, He'll walk with me.
All along my pilgrim's journey
I know Jesus will walk with me.

They were saying that Jesus was a present reality provid-ing the impetus, support, and direction for their journey. Whatever the slave community understood about Jesus, they believed He transmitted to their present experience something they could count on as continuous reality as they moved from slavery to freedom, regardless of the difficulty of the journey. It was the experience of slavery which never allowed the Black church to get caught up in the theological and philosophical meaning of Jesus, be-cause in Black religion Jesus was a practical deliverer of the oppressed. Neither, however, did they allow this temporal emphasis to decrease the understanding and appreciation of the deity of Christ.

While White preachers and theologians often defined Jesus Christ as a spiritual Savior, the deliverer of people from personal sin and guilt, Black preachers were unques-tionably historical as well. They viewed God as the Liberator in history. Thus, the Black church was very his-torical in its Christological perspective.

The Black church saw in Jesus one who suffered as they were suffering; one who had experienced oppression as they were experiencing oppression. Yet, they also saw one who was able, by virtue of His divine power, to overcome the chains of enslavement. The acts and deeds of Jesus' life and ministry were literal acts and deeds designed to provoke trust and commitment in the midst of present calamity, as the slave songs clearly demonstrated. For example,

This Man Jesus

Jesus walked the water and so raised the dead

He made the meats for those saints--He multiplied the
  bread

The blinded eyes he opened and cleansed the lepers
  too.

Then died to save sinners--Now what more could
  Jesus do?

Chorus

This man never will leave you--This man will not
  deceive you.

This man waits to relieve you--when troubles are
  bearing you down.

Oh this man when danger is near you--This man is
  ready to cheer you.

This man will always be near you--He is a wonderful
  Savior I've found.

This song shows the Black church's perception of Jesus
as actually involved in the liberation process in His earthly
life (stanza), as well as transcending what occurs now for
those who know Him. This illustrates how the "was-ness"
and "is-ness" of Jesus is wedded in the Black religious
experience.

Harold Carter argues in his book, *The Prayer Tradition of
Black People*, that the New Testament provided the slave
community with a Christ with whom they could identify.
He says, "The slave found in the person of Jesus, a savior,
a friend, and fellow sufferer at the hands of unjust oppres-
sors, who would do anything but fail."[5] Carter continues, "Doctrines about his theological nature were subor-
dinate to this pragmatic power in life. He was experienced
as a savior and a friend. There was no human condition
that Jesus could not meet."[6]

At this point, the question naturally arises as to how the
slaves became so amenable to the Savior of those who used
Him to enhance Black enslavement. The answer is found
in the slaves' African past. In the African religion, God was

so high that it took a plethora of mediators to help men reach God. Thus, virtually everything, both inanimate and animate or dead and alive, in the African religion was called upon to help the African reach the most high God and he still fell short.

However, when the slaves were confronted with the mediator Jesus Christ, they found in Him the solution to the greatest problem they ever faced in their religious experience. For with Christ, no other mediator was needed to get to God. The slaves no longer needed any subdeities.

Since Christ was the God-man, the slaves not only solved their divine problem, namely, access to the high God, but they also solved a very historical problem as well. Perfect humanity provided the slaves with someone who could liberate them in history from any and every kind of problem, injustice, and oppression. Sadly enough, this aspect of Christ's work was ignored and misunderstood by the broader Christian society. Carter agrees that traditional religion from West Africa gave Blacks an orientation that allowed them to adapt easily to Jesus. Because in African Traditional Religion there was the role of the divine mediator, it was permanent and natural to accept this Christ who could bring God down to the slaves. Carter explains,

> With such a background of this and similar African deities, it was not hard for Black people to assign to Jesus literal powers. He "came in my sick room." He "cooled scorching fever and calmed troubled minds." He was a "heart fixer and mind regulator." He was a "lawyer in the courtroom, doctor in the sick room, friend to the friendless, husband to the widow, mother to the motherless, and father to the fatherless." He saved from sin, had power over the "devil," and guided his children with his eye. All these basic deeds were continually attributed to him in prayer.7

The reason that prayer could be made to Jesus in this manner is because His earthly life and ministry demonstrated that He cared and had the power to make a difference.

Thus, the Black church saw the teaching of the New Testament, combined with the reality of the Black religious experience, as validating the existence and meaning of its Christological system, since both affirmed Christ as Savior from personal sin as well as deliverer of the oppressed.

From a biblical perspective, the natural question here is not only can human liberation be demonstrated to be part and parcel of Jesus' ministry, but also can He be demonstrated to be the very ground of human liberation as Black religion asserts? The answer is an unqualified yes on both counts.

The Old Testament serves as the basis for understanding the ministry of Christ in the New Testament. The concerns of liberation in the New Testament that are expressed by Jesus Christ must naturally take their clue from the Old Testament perceptions of those concerns. In the Old Testament, spiritual salvation and human liberation were intricately linked. Faith and obedience automatically brought blessings and protection from the enemy, while unbelief and disobedience brought cursing and captivity. The categorical imperative of Moses in his final message to Israel was obey and live or disobey and die (Deut. 28). A proper relationship to Yahweh automatically assumed that there was to be a proper relationship to the covenant community. Therefore, the Ten Commandments are divided between Israel's relationship to God and to each other.

Jesus' understanding of this Old Testament relationship between divine salvation and human liberation is expressed in Matthew 22:35-40 where Jesus is asked by a lawyer,"Teacher, which is the great commandment in the Law?" (v. 36). His single question received a dual answer; Jesus responded,"'You shall love the Lord your God with all your heart, and with all your soul, and with all your mind.' This is the great and foremost commandment. The second is like it, 'You shall love your neighbor as yourself.' On these two commandments depend the whole Law and the Prophets" (vv. 37-40). In Jesus' answer, a number of things are to be noticed.

The first feature, and of primary importance to the question of liberation, is the fact that a person's proper relationship to our neighbor is placed on a similar level with our love for God as far as having a proper perception of the meaning of revelation in the Law and the Prophets. That is, a proper perception of the content and meaning of the Law and the Prophets is based not only on a person's relationship to God, but also on whether we are rightly related to our neighbor. The implication is that any understanding of what it means to love God that does not also express itself in love for neighbor cannot provide the student of the Old Testament with a proper perception of the meaning of Scripture. To perceive the Old Testament rightly there must be a proper relationship to both God and man.

A question that might be raised at this point is: does love of our neighbor automatically assume involvement in human liberation? The answer is yes for three reasons:

1.) The meaning of love your neighbor in the Law and the Prophets included keeping and relieving him from oppression. This is why the context of the Old Testament reference that Jesus uses from Leviticus 19:18 includes not oppressing your neighbor. For example, Leviticus 19:13 reads, "You shall not oppress your neighbor, nor rob him." Again, verse 15 reads, "You shall not be partial to the poor nor defer to the great, but you are to judge your neighbor fairly."

2.) Jesus' own definition of neighbor is based on the idea of aiding a person who has undergone acts of oppression. When the question was put to Jesus in Luke 10:29, "Who is my neighbor?" Jesus answered by relating a story of a man who had fallen among thieves and was left to die. The method Jesus used to distinguish who was the true neighbor was comparing those who saw this man's condition and ignored it with the Samaritan who provided the man relief from his oppressive circumstance. Jesus' point was that our neighbor is the one whose need we see and whose need we are able to meet (Luke 10:30-37). Thus, Jesus saw the condition of oppression as intrinsic to a proper perception of defining the meaning of neighbor.

3.) The New Testament, like the Old Testament, singles out the poor and oppressed as special objects of God's love and concern. Jesus understood his own call to be a ministry to the poor and oppressed (Luke 4:18, 19). The church is expected to have that same sensitivity to the oppressed. James writes, "Did not God choose the poor of this world to be rich in faith and heirs of the kingdom which He promised to those who love Him?" (James 2:5). Thus, love for our neighbor must give special attention to those who are the poor and oppressed of society. James also defines true religion by how we treat the widows and orphans (James 1:27).

A second feature of Jesus' response concerning the greatest of the commandments is that both commandments call for the identical commitment of love. In both cases, the Greek word is *agape*, meaning "to love." Since the meaning of biblical love is "that which seeks the will of God in the object loved," then it can be concluded that the same intensity commanded of us to submit to God's will (heart, soul, mind) is also the same intensity that we are to have in order to assure that our neighbor experiences God's will operating in his life.

Thus, the love factor means our relationship to God involves not only a commitment to and experience of God, but also our participation in assuring that our neighbor experiences that same kind of love. Certainly, this automatically excludes any possibility of oppression being justified, since loving our neighbor includes relieving him from oppression.

This point is emphasized by the Apostle John when he says, "If someone says, 'I love God,' and hates his brother, he is a liar; for the one who does not love his brother whom he has seen, cannot love God whom he has not seen" (1 John 4:20). Therefore, when Jesus includes the second commandment and says it is like the first, He is saying that love for God cannot be validated apart from love of others. Such love, John reminds us, is not only to be expressed in words, but also "in deed and truth" (1 John 3:18).

There is a third feature in Jesus' response that must be brought to bear on the question of human liberation. While it is true that the vertical and horizontal relationships are two sides of the same coin, the latter is the outgrowth of the former. That is, in the mind of Jesus, our relationship with God is the basis upon which there can be a proper relationship with man. That is seen in two ways.

First, after quoting Deuteronomy 6:5, Jesus indicates that love for God is the answer to the question of which commandment was greatest prior to introducing the second commandment. The fact that He uses the same Greek word "great," *megale*, that the lawyer used to define which commandment takes priority demonstrates that in the mind of Jesus love for God was the basis upon which love for your neighbor could be expressed.

The second way is the addition of the word *prote*, which means "first"; its usage here designates "first in rank or degree." Thus Jesus, in the addition of *prote*, ranks the degree of love one has for God as the foundational basis and motivation for a proper understanding of love for our neighbor.

Jesus, then, is the foundation for liberation to the extent that liberation is based on a proper response to God. This is not to say that He condones oppression when that oppression exists apart from a proper relationship with God. Rather, it says that Jesus' participation in the process of human liberation is a particular outgrowth of our relationship with God. This means that the Black church was on strong theological footing in seeing in Christ the basis for liberation from oppression in history. While such recognition was not understood in highly technical exegetical formulas, it was nonetheless biblically sound and the clearest and earliest expression of this Christological theme in America.

The strengths of this Christological understanding of the historical Black church is not only instructional for the limited scope of the White church, but it is also equally instructional for the social weaknesses of the contemporary Black church as well. Israel was an oppressed community in the New Testament because it was in bondage to Rome. Their Christology took them to the point that they recognized Jesus as the one with the message of the Kingdom and the power to miraculously relieve their condition of oppression. Yet, when they sought to make Him king (John 6:15), He refused. The problem was that a Christology that only leads to political, social, and economic reform is an insufficient Christology. Human liberation must always be predicated on spiritual salvation. This is why Jesus said, "Repent, for the kingdom of heaven is at hand" (Matt. 4:17), and why he told Nicodemus, "Unless one is born again, he cannot see the kingdom of God" (John 3:3).

Along with being predicated on spiritual salvation, human liberation is to be predicated on a willingness to obey Christ as master. Thus, the process of liberation must be willing to incorporate the principles of Christ if it would present Christ as the leader of the struggle. This is why Jesus said to His followers, "And why do you call Me, 'Lord, Lord,' and do not do what I say?" (Luke 6:46).

Applying this to the Black experience means that it is improper Christology to say that Christ is leading the struggle against American racism if He is not first enthroned in the lives of those involved in leading the liberation struggle. To the degree that the Black experience expresses the liberation motif as a natural extension of the activity of Christ acting in the hearts and lives of those who have trusted Him as Savior and obeying Him as Lord, there is a basis for a correct Christological statement. But the fact that liberation is taking place under the banner of Jesus Christ is not a sufficient enough statement in and of itself. The leadership must possess both a proper saving relationship to Christ and proper biblical methodology before the Black church can ever return to the position of strength it has experienced in the past.

THE COMMUNAL NATURE OF THE BLACK CHURCH

The Black church viewed itself as more than just a loose gathering of individuals. It saw itself as a community in which everyone was related. This communal mind set again owed its existence to the African world view. In Africa, tribal life was family life, and family life was also religious life. Idowu comments,

> The household grew into the compound--which is usually an oblong or circular enclosure of houses with a common space in the middle and made up in the main of the family which has been extended through procreation, through the living together of blood relations, and the addition to them of"strangers" who came or were brought to dwell among them. In such a compound, there is in the central house, a shrine which is dedicated to the common ancestor. Worship here is undertaken by the supreme head of the extended family who is"father" or"grandfather" to the whole community. The whole community is the offspring of the ancestor as well as of the central tutelary divinity. This supreme head is entitled to his priestly function because he is the senior of the blood relations in the extended family and therefore succeeds to the priestly function which used to belong to the common ancestor from whom the family descended.[8]

Within the tribal clan people found support, affirmation, protection, and guidance. All of these things were experienced in a context of love with God at the center of tribal life. The Black church also provided a context for the redefinition of the slave in terms of God rather than the society in which he now lived. In church he was perpetually reminded of who he was from the divine perspective. One who was considered a boy on the plantation became Deacon Jones on Sunday. An elderly woman who would be known as a girl during the week by her mistress would become Mother Smith in church. The church, then, was crucial for maintaining God's view of Black dignity and significance under the hand of a good God.

Therefore, when the slaves came to America, the new tribe, of which God was the center, was the Black church. Rather than accepting the broader society's definition of the church, which oftentimes lacked a communal life orientation, they reached back to their African understanding of family which became the basis for the functioning of the Black church. This communal perspective of the church was reflected in how people related to each other, as uncle, cousin, brother or sister. This perspective was also responsible for the Black church being a successful beneficial brotherhood that took care of its sick, supported its widows and orphans, educated its children, and developed its independent financial base.

The parallel between the motif in Scripture and the communal emphasis of the Black church was obvious. The fact that the church is to be viewed as a community, that is, a group of individuals inseparably linked together, can be seen clearly in a number of ways. The family emphasis of the New Testament demonstrates its community nature. The church is referred to as the household of faith (Gal. 6:10), God's household (Eph. 2:19; 1 Pet. 4:17), a spiritual house (1 Pet. 2:5), and believers are viewed as fellow citizens (Eph. 2:19), and members of one another (Rom. 12:5; Eph. 4:25).

The church is further seen as a tightly knitted community by the emphasis on its unity and oneness. Although it is made up of many members, it is one body (1

Cor. 12:20) that suffers together (1 Cor. 12:26) and is fitly joined together and compacted (Eph. 4:16). Because all of its *pneumatic* gifts come from one Lord, there is to be no schism in the one body (1 Cor. 12:3-5, 25-31).

Internally, the first church "began selling their property and possessions, and were sharing them with all, as anyone might have need" (Acts 2:45). This was a voluntary act of the church to meet each other's needs so that there would be no unnecessary physical suffering. While the New Testament does not make it imperative that the church use the same method of sharing, the New Testament is quite clear that such sharing within the church is the obligation of the church so that the physical needs of its members are met.

The church is commanded to meet the physical needs of its members in the provision of money for poor believers (Acts 11:17-30; Rom. 15:25, 27; 2 Cor. 8:1-24), clothing (James 2:15), and the world's goods in general (1 John 3:17). Such meeting of needs can be both individual (James 2:15) and corporate (2 Cor. 8:18-22). Those who are to benefit from the church's internal outreach are those who are not the well-to-do of society, such as the widows who have no foreseeable means of support (1 Tim. 5:9, 10), orphans (James 1:27), and the poor (1 John 3:17).

The reason why the church is to be particularly sensitive to those who do not have the world's goods is that God has placed a priority on giving them rich faith and future rewards. James 2:5 says, "Listen, my beloved brethren: did not God choose the poor of this world to be rich in faith and heirs of the kingdom which He promised to those who love Him?" This passage is important for the present discussion because it sets forth the divine value God gives to the poor in the church. Since God gives the earthly poor great spiritual riches, namely, faith and future reward, it is an insult to God's value system to treat the poor in an inferior way. The church then must reflect towards the poor the value that God gives them.

It is important to note that the poor are not said to be chosen because they are poor, nor are all the poor chosen (Rev. 13:16). The poor that are chosen are done so with the goal of developing their spiritual riches.

Another point to be made here is that James can still refer to the rich Christians who are dishonoring the poor as"beloved brethren," only because their sin of oppression has nothing necessarily to do with the fact of salvation. They were at the same time brethren and"judges with evil motives" (James 2:4). This demonstrates that oppression is nothing new to the church, although such activity is condemned by God and should be vigorously resisted.

Another reason James gives for prioritizing ministry to the poor of the church is the normalcy of the oppression of the poor by the rich (James 2:6). Therefore, the church is to be both conscious of and functionally beneficial to those who are the oppressed and poor of the church.

The church also has a secondary social responsibility to the broader non-Christian society (Gal. 6:10). While this does not receive the specificity that the internal responsibility does, it is nevertheless the responsibility of the church to"speak the truth" to the whole culture with regard to God's perspective regarding the oppressed. Peter's statement to the Sanhedrin that"we must obey God rather than men" (Acts 5:29) says that whenever a religious or civil ruling body (since the Sanhedrin was both)[9] contradicts what God has said or commanded, disobedience to that body is justified.

Peter's response was"a statement made with respect to disobeying the command of the Sanhedrin, which had not only religious power but also wide political power at that time."[10] God has commanded the church to be"equitable" and honest in its dealings with unbelievers (1 Pet. 2:12), to work honest labor to sustain one's self (1 Thess. 4:11, 12), to be hospitable to strangers (Heb. 13:2), to practice justice and fairness (Col. 4:1), and to hold no social distinctions (James 2:1). Therefore, if society or religion or government ignores or thwarts efforts to obey these commands, the believer and the church have a basis for godly, biblically-based rebellion.

In addition, when the government fails to fulfill its divine responsibility of promoting justice (Rom. 13:1-5), then Christians have the right and responsibility to resist, as long as such resistance is within the parameters that correspond with proper Christian behavior. Paul exhibited an act of civil disobedience when he refused to obey the command of the chief magistrates of Philippi when they asked him to leave jail after he had been illegally beaten.[11] Such an act was justified, however, because the civil authority was unjust. Paul "was trying by legitimate means to compel the Roman authorities to fulfill their God-appointed task. It is to be noted that he did not stage his sit-in because of some selfish personal claim against the authorities."[12]

The Black church, then, stands on solid biblical ground as a liberating community. However, that ground is only as solid as its biblical moorings. While the contemporary church still possesses the responsive cord of biblical liberation, it is far too often out of tune with biblical methodology. Such a conspicuous absence is one of the primary reasons for the weaknesses now plaguing Black America.

If the Black church, for example, would apply our historical, biblical understanding of God's promise to be a mother to the motherless and father to the fatherless (Ps. 27:10; 131:1-3; 146:9), then there would be no Black children caught in overcrowded, state-run adoption agencies. These children would be properly raised in the secure and loving environment of families supplied by the church. Such a contemporary application by the Black church of the true meaning of God's promise of parenthood through the care and concern of mothers and fathers in the church would also show the broader society how to address social issues through the private sector.

This same biblical approach should be used to address all the problems we face, including housing, employment, and education. Just as the historical Black church was the spiritual hub that connected the community spokes of Black- owned and operated businesses, the Black press, Black colleges, and community-based mutual aid societies, even so today we can function in that same role. The Black church can again be that hub which turns the wheels of Black community development and revitalization, as well as be the foundation for racial reconciliation in America.

The state of the Black community at large is merely a reflection of the failure or success of the church. By reviewing and applying the strengths of our biblical and historical heritage, we can reverse the negative conditions in our community while simultaneously helping the White church to come to grips with a major biblical theme that it has allowed to slip through its grasp.

Notes--Chapter 4

[1]Henry H. Mitchell, *Black Belief*, p. 109.

[2]See William Banks, *The Black Church in the U.S.*, p. 17, for a summary of the influence of the Great Awakening on the slaves.

[3]See John Lovell Jr., *Black Song: The Forge and the Flame*, for a comprehensive understanding of the music of the slave community.

[4]"Story" in Black religious tradition refers to the progressive activity of God within the Black community whereby He works in and through them, in keeping with His biblical movement in the deliverance of Israel and development of the church, to bring about their personal and collective salvation and liberation.

[5]Harold A. Carter, *The Prayer Tradition of Black People*, p. 47.

[6]Ibid.
[7]Ibid., p. 48.

[8]E. Bolaji Idowu, *Olòdúmarè God in Yoruba Belief*, p. 131.

[9]D. A. Hagner explains this dual role of the Sanhedrin when he says,"The Sanhedrin certainly had complete control of the religious affairs of the nation as the Mishnah indicates. The high court was the supreme authority in the interpretation of the Mosaic Law, and when it mediated in questions disputed in the lower courts, its verdict was final. Beyond this, the Sanhedrin also governed civil affairs and tried certain criminal cases under the authority of the Roman procurator. The Romans were quite content to let subject nations regulate internal affairs, but there were, of course, always limits. They, for example, would have reserved the right to intervene at will."

Thus Hagner says,"The Sanhedrin had every right to prosecute Jesus for alleged crimes whether religious or civil." (D. A. Hagner,"Sanhedrin," *Zondervan Pictorial Encyclopedia of the Bible*, 5 vols., v:271, 272.)

[10]Charles C. Ryrie,"Perspective on Social Ethics," *Bibliotheca Sacra*: 316.

[11]F. F. Bruce explains why this beating was illegal."Even if condemned a Roman citizen was exempt from flogging. By the Valerian and Porcian Laws (passed at various times between 509 and 195 B.C.) Roman citizens were exempted from all degrading forms of punishment (e.g., beating with rods, scourging, crucifixion)." *The Acts of the Apostles*, p. 322.

[12]Ryrie, p. 316.

Chapter 5

The Role of the Black Preacher

Since the Black church emerged in a context of oppression and slavery which helped shape it into the primary institution of liberation and survival for Black people, it stands to reason that the emergence of the Black preacher would also reflect this same contextual significance.

The failure both to understand and appreciate the Black preacher in slavery is ultimately a failure to take seriously the existential reality of American slavery and its comprehensive social impact on the slaves. When we understand that social realities demanded that the Black church as an institution had to, of necessity, be a community of liberation, then we can concurrently appreciate the fact that the Black preacher had to be the leader of the liberation movement.

Such an understanding transforms our view and value of the Black preacher from being a mere religious figurehead into being an architect of freedom. When seen in this light one wonders how the Black preacher could achieve so much with so little. The marvel is that he could be so theological without having any formal theological training. His Christianity coupled with his African history world view enabled him to aptly engineer the survival of his people as well as sketch the plan to overcome the laws, systems, and errant theology of the broader American culture. The presence of the Black preacher also demonstrated in visual fashion the biblical theme of justice. His presence as leader of the Black church forced a moral consciousness upon the broader society that it would not have had without his leadership.

THE EMERGENCE OF THE BLACK PREACHER

Similar to the Black church, the Black preacher finds his roots in the African Traditional Religion. As has been stated, African religion is folk religion. It finds its chief expression in and through the oral and life communications of the members of the tribal community. The priest in these tribal communities was characterized by his ability to remember the proverbs and stories (Odu) and communicate them to the members of the tribe in an accurate and effective manner, providing them with a link between their past and their present. The priest, then, was the embodiment of the history, culture, and heritage of the tribe! H. Beecher Hicks says,

> The vast power of the priest in the African state is well known; his realm alone--the province of religion and medicine--remained largely unaffected by the plantation system. The Negro priest, therefore, early became an important figure on the plantation and found his function as the interpreter of the supernatural, the comforter of the sorrowing, and as the one who expressed, rudely but picturesquely, the longing and disappointment and resentment of a stolen people.[1]

It should be little wonder that the Black preacher has perpetually served as a father figure to Black people, seeing to their welfare in all spheres of life whether they were social, political, economic, or the traditionally recognized spiritual aspects of life. Such a position is not unknown to biblical revelation. The New Testament church leaders had little trouble viewing their followers from a parent-child perspective. Thus Paul could call Timothy his son (2 Tim. 1:2) and Titus his child (Titus 1:4). John could call Christians he was teaching his children (1 John 2:1, 12) and even explain their various spiritual statuses within the framework of the different levels within the family structure, namely, fathers, young men, and children (1 John 2:13-14).

Here again the African past prepared the preacher well for his posture within the Christian church. While this parental role has at times been abused by some Black preachers, it has also served as the driving force behind the development and survival of the Black church, in much the same way as the Apostle Paul's loving yet firm parental role did for the church at Thessalonica (1 Thess. 2:7-12).

The African priestly heritage also explains the posture of the preacher as spiritual representative of Black people before God. Since God is viewed as a comprehensive part of all of life, the Black preacher has traditionally represented God's presence and leadership in every part of Black life. This fact also explains the dominant place announcements have played in Black church worship, sometimes taking as much time as the sermon. Since God was the center of all of life, then Sunday morning would be used to relate Him to every aspect of the community. The announcement period facilitated the wedding between the priest, oral tradition, community life, and the centrality of God, allowing them to converge in the context of the worship experience. The Black worship context provided the preacher a weekly platform with which to guide his people in the comprehensive application of faith to life. The community grapevine would assure that what was announced on Sunday would get disseminated on Monday.

The presence of the priest also provided cohesiveness for the tribe or clan. He served as the point person for the African relationship with one another, as well as their individual and collective relationship with God. He led them in their ceremonies and festivals which reflected the essence of tribal life and served as the basis for the world view of the community in microcosmic form.

When the slaves arrived on the plantations they had lost neither their desire nor their need for the social cohesion they had known in Africa. In fact, they desired it even more in light of the extreme isolation from the broader society they were experiencing. However, there was no social cohesion apart from the priest, the divine representative of the community. The Black preacher filled this role in the context of Christianity. Black churches were now the new clans and the Black preacher was the new priest. Since access to formal religious structures of the broader society were virtually non-existent, Black preachers were relatively free to draw intuitively on their African past for many of the ingredients that would become normative aspects of Black worship. Mitchell says,

> The preaching tradition of the Black Fathers did not spring into existence suddenly. It was developed after a long and often quite disconnected series of contacts between the Christian gospel variously interpreted and men caught up in the Black experience of slavery and oppression. To this experience and this gospel they brought their own culture and folkways. In ways more unique and powerful than they or we dreamed until recently, they developed a Black religious tradition. Very prominent in that Black religious tradition were Black-culture sermons and the ways Black men delivered and responded to them.[2]

The varied and small gatherings that were part of the developing invisible institution of the Black church required and allowed for the emergence of the Black preacher. They required the emergence of the Black preacher because African traditional religion required the presence of the priest for the spiritual and social linkage of the people to each other as well as to God. His emergence was allowed because even within the broader White Christian structure there existed the position of pastor who was responsible for providing spiritual leadership to local congregations. Therefore, as these new clan gatherings developed, the roles of the African priest and the Christian pastor merged in the rise of the Black preacher.

The psychological, social, and spiritual needs of the slave community dictated that the preacher be someone who demonstrated the greatest leadership qualities in communicating to the people and on behalf of the people in their freedom quest. The Black preacher had significant contact with Whites and therefore was in the unique position to learn, analyze, and interpret their ways. His knowledge then had to be communicated to the slave community in such a way as to simultaneously teach the slave about God, protect the slave against oppression, lead the community into a dualistic understanding of freedom (temporal and eternal), and stay within the framework of the social and religious boundaries of the slave master. It should thus be obvious why the cream of the crop rose to the position of Black preacher.

Because of the oral predisposition of the slave preacher, neither he nor the developing Black church were hampered in their pursuit of the God of justice because of limited access to academic training. This is the only way to explain how there existed the perpetual dissemination of the great Christian themes in spite of the denial of even an elementary level of education.

The Bible became the authoritative source book for the preacher and his congregation's developing understanding of God and their quest for freedom. However, the

Bible was not used as a means of developing an esoteric epistomology (the study of the origin, nature, methods, and limits of knowledge). It was a tool for understanding and directing the Black Christian community through its experience of oppression. When the Black preacher opened his Bible, it was more for the interpretation of recent experience than for detailed exegetical analysis. There was no such thing as the impersonal use of the Bible. The different preaching styles between the Black and White preacher were not primarily related to a lack of expositional ability. It was related to an ethical rather than epistomological orientation to life.

It must be concluded that the Black preacher, rather than being inferior, was exceptional with his ability to lead, communicate, memorize, interpret the times, and link the past with the present. To think that he was able to do this with little or no formal education, opposition from the broader culture, and little money, while still addressing the personal needs of the members of the community, is nothing short of a miracle. This fact in and of itself should dispel any notion of Black inferiority and may, to the contrary, be an argument for the scholarship of Black preachers in the realm of applied theology.

THE LEADERSHIP OF THE BLACK PREACHER

Since the dawn of the Black man in the Western Hemisphere, the spiritual, social, and political leaders of the Black community have been one and the same. In the Black community, the separation of church and state was taboo. The secular had to remain sacred because of the plight of the people. This reality was very normal and comfortable for the slave community with its African wholistic world view.

Because of the existence of oppression, racism and other social maladies, there was a need for spiritual strength amid the social climate. The tie between the fight for social emancipation and the demand for divine justice were irreversibly intertwined. Thus, when it came to leadership in the Black community, the concern for social justice and spiritual fortitude warranted the place and role of the preacher. In him resided all the attributes required to wage the war for justice. He was the pillar of the community worthy of the utmost respect.

The scenario in the Black community was seen as the modern expression of Israel. And like their Jewish brothers of the past, the plight of the African slaves was thwarted by the oppressive yoke of slavery. When the African slave looked at the saga of the Jewish people from Exodus through the Book of Joshua, he saw himself. Moreover, deep in the recesses of his heart he knew that the same God who broke the yoke of slavery for Israel could do the same for him.

Thus, the slave structured his mental and spiritual framework to complement that of ancient Israel. His leaders had to be spiritual and political. Just as the dilemma of Israel required Moses and Joshua to be great spiritual, political, and military leaders, so it was in the African-American community. This perspective of leadership produced leaders like Martin Luther King, Jr., Jesse Jackson, and Richard Allen. The African-American community believed it was involved in a Jihad, "Holy War." And thus only those considered to be holy men could be at the helm. Even when Malcolm X emerged in the 1960s, he did so from the platform of a minister, albeit Muslim, but nevertheless a religious figure.

It was the holocaust of slavery that forged this union of priest and presiding officer, but it was the continuance of oppression that fostered and fed this need for the man of God to lead the way. As the Black historian Charles V. Hamilton remarks,

> And so it has been throughout the history of Black people in America. The Black preacher has been called upon by politicians, parishioners, peacemakers and all others. He has been the

natural leader in the Black community. He has a
fixed base, the church; he has a perpetual con-
stituency, the congregation, which he sees as-
sembled for at least one or two hours a week,
then the preacher's contact far exceeds one or
two hours.[3]

The key word which summarizes the leadership role of
the Black preacher is "link." He has had the perpetual
responsibility of tying together the old with the new. This
is clearly demonstrated on the four cataclysmic cultural
transformations Black people have experienced[4]: 1) the
transition from African freedom to American slavery; 2)
the transition from American slavery to American freedom
during Reconstruction; 3) the transition from the South to
the North during and following World War I; 4) and finally
the transition from segregation to integration during the
civil rights movement.

Such a leadership role is often characterized and perceived as inferior because it majors on the social and political aspects of life rather than the theological and spiritual.
Such a position, however, results from a limited and faulty
criteria. There were aspects that were inferior, not because
they were social or political, but because the method used
did not always reflect biblical methodology or salvific
purposes. Similarly, White preachers who vehemently
"contended for the faith" in their legitimate war against the
onslaught of liberalism during the early part of the twentieth century did not reflect biblical methodology in the
maintenance of racism, segregationism, and classism.

The problem in both cases is a failure to be thoroughly
biblical, for God gives clear theological guidelines to go-
vern the social and political issues of life. Because it was
not understood that Black preachers were simply bringing
another issue to the theological table that needed to be
"contended for," it was written off as social, not spiritual,
and therefore by definition, inferior. The refusal of the
church in America to address the issue of race gave rise to

the Black preacher's expertise in this theological arena. It has also led to the White church recognizing, at the end of the twentieth century, that the Black church and its leader, the Black preacher, were truly the experts in this forgotten field of theology.

The issues of slavery and racism were not merely matters of politics and states rights. They were a matter of what was right before God. There was nothing Christian about the dehumanization of one man by another. Where the Bible says, "Love your neighbor as yourself" (James 2:8), it means just that! There is nothing neighborly about subjecting a person to something that you would detest. Furthermore, where the Bible is a strong advocate of the family and fidelity in marriage, slave owners used the mating process (which God had given mankind to make more image-bearers) as a tool for breeding stock as though the slave owners were trying to produce the next Derby winner.

The very institution of slavery in America was unbiblical. It was imperative that the Black preacher voice his concerns as a political activist but, more importantly, as a man of God on this theological issue. For such was the role of a prophet.

Although Blacks were no longer wearing iron shackles after the civil war, the shackles were still there. The new shackles were now set in writing: "Whites Only" or "Colored Rest Rooms Here." The Massa (Master) had also changed. He now wore a suit and the whip was his ability to deny access to opportunity and equality. Just as the early slave preachers were to lead their people to freedom, even so in contemporary America the task remains the same.

Thus, the leadership role of the Black preacher, from slavery to the present, has remained constant. Such a consistent posture is not the mark of an inferior people, but rather a determined people. We are a people who see in the character of God a scarlet thread called justice which is so strong that it can keep a people focused and a leadership baton passing from generation to generation without wavering.

THE UNIQUENESS OF BLACK PREACHING

In the Black religious experience, preaching is much more than one man sharing the Word with the congregation. Preaching is an event.[5] Preaching in the Black church thrives on the participation of the congregation. Sermons are not unilateral but bilateral. The term bilateral refers to the discourse going on between the preacher and the audience (known as the "call and response pattern"). The preacher initiates the conversation and the congregation answers back both verbally and with gestures. For example, when someone in the audience raises his hand or says "amen!" to a point in the sermon, it serves as a communique to the preacher that the message or impact of his comment was received. The preacher, the Bible, and the congregation are all intertwined in a rich interpersonal theological discourse.

I remember having a prominent Black evangelical pastor in Dallas speak at Oak Cliff Bible Fellowship. You could feel the conversation going on between himself and the congregation. Toward the end of the sermon the pace of his speech began to slow down. You could tell that the interpersonal atmosphere was about to take a leap into the ionosphere of communication. The critical juncture was when he introduced the statement, "When I think about the cross." The point was the word "I." The whole episode was ripe for this exchange of personal testimony. Not only was the truth of the cross true because it was in the Bible, but it was true as well because God had born witness of its monumental impact in the preacher's life.

This was not just a sermon. This was not simply a transfer of ideology from one man to a group of people. This was a verbal celebration of God and all of His glory. This preacher was saying that his own eyes had seen the glory of the cross and now he was ready to bear witness of it. Black preaching is a dynamic conversation between the preacher, the congregation, and the Bible which celebrates the immaculate splendor, holiness, and power of God.

The Black preacher did not learn his craft in a classroom. It was the actual church service that served as his classroom. In other words, it was caught prior to being taught. Thus the method of instruction employed to train him was existential. Preaching was learned through experiencing it. It was easy because he was already predisposed by his heritage to receive it this way.

One of the problems with many Black seminarians today is that preaching for them is often reduced to an academic exercise. That which has always been natural for the Black preacher is often programmed for him in evangelical institutions, with the tragic result that many exit seminary having lost their ability to preach. Black preaching is thirsty for zest. And it is this zest that the Black congregation will demand. If there is not lively, earthy appeal in the sermon, it can become difficult to preach to a Black congregation. And you cannot be a Black preacher and not preach. The uniqueness of the Black preacher is born out of his cultural orientation. It is not a fair trade for him to gain exegetical prowess and then lose the attention of his audience.

Many homiletics departments in evangelical seminaries view the emotionalism involved in Black liturgy as superfluous. This is due to an insufficient understanding of the value of the worship experience in the Black church as well as the nature of biblical worship. At the core of biblical worship is the celebration of God for who He is and what He has done. When we observe the portraits of worship painted throughout the Old Testament, spoken about in the Psalms, and prophesied in heaven in the Book of Revelation, we do not see passive environments where the people sit as spectators while the professionals perform. Rather, the whole congregation is called to worship God using every element of expression from shouting, to dancing, to praising, to crying.

It is this celebrative aspect of worship that has even caught on among middle and upper classes within the White community with the rise of the Charismatic movement. What has become new in the White community regarding the celebrative nature of worship has been normative for Black worship throughout its history. This again demonstrates the fallacy of the notion that Black worship is inferior. In fact, Black worship seems tame when compared with many of the emotional excesses among some Charismatics.

However, there is a danger in Black preaching and Black worship that overemphasizes emotion and performance. If we lose our audience amid a storm of confusion, "every wind of doctrine" will blow in. Culture is the vehicle, not the driver. The focus of worship must always be the presentation of truth whether it is sung, taught, or preached. May it never be that we glorify the package with its pretty wrapping while ignoring the precious treasure inside. This is why the Black preacher must be a good expositor, as well as a good storyteller.

Conversely we cannot camouflage bad expository preaching by casting the bread of Greek and Hebrew words onto the waters of the congregation. Academics cannot cover up bad preaching. Neither should the presentation of the truth resemble a documentary on some little-known subject on the Public Broadcasting Channel. The best scenario is to fuse the uniqueness of Black preaching with strong biblical exegesis. Therefore, the preacher should be both interesting and exacting. Surely it's a crime to bore people with the Word of God, a crime very few Black preachers would ever be convicted of.

Historically, the Black preacher is tied to the priority of oral communication. He focused on retention rather than using notes in the pulpit. This tradition evolved out of a couple of factors. The first factor is his African heritage which focused on oral communication and retention. The second factor is that for years the Black preacher was barred from entering the seminaries that taught preaching as a technical process. Thus the Black preacher simply maintained his heritage which gave him a great deal of success in his venue.

In Africa, story telling is used to paint pictures of life. The whole culture, its history and its essence, is preserved through oral tradition and celebrative rituals. Story telling is also put to melodies and expressed in song.

Since the Bible is over two-thirds narrative, the Black preacher is right at home with this type of material. Deuteronomy 6 advocates oral communication as an excellent way to transfer the truth of God to our children. "And these words, which I am commanding you today, shall be on your heart; and you shall teach them diligently to your sons and shall talk of them when you sit in your house and when you walk by the way and when you lie down and when you rise up" (Deut. 6:6-7). This is similar to African oral tradition, which naturally expressed truth in the normal movement of life.

The Bible was the first book the slave learned, but in the majority of cases it was not because he could read it. He learned it through what he heard and began interpreting life through it. The Black preacher used the Bible to interpret life for himself and his people. Even when slavery ended, because the Black preacher was denied access to institutions of higher learning, the Bible remained his comprehensive manual on all of life. Since Blacks did not have many educational options, they maintained a very orthodox view of Christianity. Their world view was not jaundiced by extraneous and sometimes erroneous thought patterns. The preacher, then, was in an honored position in his community because he interpreted all of life for his people.

The basis of the Black preacher's preaching was a hermeneutical theology. Hermeneutics refers to the method of biblical interpretation one uses. It's interpretational grid was life. Where biblical truth intersected with life the door to a better life both here and in the hereafter was opened.

This type of interpretational model is known as a "language event." As Richard Soulen explains,

> A language event can be said to have occurred when reality becomes efficaciously present in language. Here the appearance of "reality" is identified with the simultaneous coming into being of its "language." Without language there is no "reality."[5]

The language event scenario has advantages. This methodology alerts us to the way language is used. Thus there was always a strong tie between the reality of life and the words of the Bible. This hermeneutic was also put to melody and sung in the spirituals. Many of the "old Negro spirituals" were examples of double entendre. That is, they had a dual intent. Certainly they were speaking of religious experiences, but in the primal days of the Black slave, they were also used to encode messages about escape routes to the North. Life meets religion!

Exegesis is the process wherein hermeneutical principles are applied. The objective is to obtain the meaning of a given passage. Exegesis is done when the capacity of the reader is insufficient to produce understanding immediately. The tools of the exegete--lexicons, Greek and Hebrew grammar books, systematic theologies, etc.--serve as surrogate reservoirs of knowledge which link the exegete to the ancient culture.

The drawback in the African-American community is that traditionally the clergy, by and large, has not been trained to employ the services of such tools. The saving grace of the African-American church heretofore has been its historically evangelical stance transmitted in large part by oral tradition. In many respects, biblical interpretation is easy for the Black preacher because so many of the events of the lives of biblical personages mirror events of the Black community's struggle in America. This is a great advantage.

However, there comes a time when it is essential to probe the depths of biblical literature for a more precise meaning which may lie upon the pages of Scripture beneath the etymology of a certain word or beneath an ancient cultural innuendo. For example, in Ephesians 5:22, the word *hupotasso* ("to be subject to") is used to instruct the wife as to the nature of her relationship with her husband. The word used in Ephesians 6:1 and 6:5 to instruct children and slaves respectively to obey or submit to the will of their parents and masters is *hupakouo*. To many "would-be" biblical interpreters, an English reading of these three passages would seem to imply that the nature of the subjection is, in all three cases, the same. But this is not so.

Hupotasso, used in 5:22, is in the middle voice in Greek, and therefore carries the idea of volitional submission. The woman's submission of herself to her husband is conditioned by her relationship with the Lord, and thus she submits of her own free choice to do so, in conformity with God's elder for the household. This is not the case in 6:1 and 6:5. The word *hupakouo* is much stronger. It is used to refer to flat out obedience which does not conflict with other biblical guidelines, since both the slave and the master are to give flat out obedience to God first. Thus when the parent tells the child to jump, the child's response is, "When, Sir, and how high would you like me to jump?"

Furthermore, there is the issue of the word "slave" in this passage, which was not at all the same kind of slavery as was instituted in America. Slaves during the first century were not merely chattel but were considered as part of the household. Also, slaves were not denied access to learning. Many slaves were their master's tutors in such areas as philosophy, history, rhetoric, and law.

Moreover the context of Ephesians 5:21-6:9 is governed by Paul's imperative in 5:18 which commands that Christians "be filled," or better translated, "be under the influence of the Holy Spirit." The idea of "being controlled" is a much better expression in the English language to convey what Paul was trying to urge us to do. The Greek word *pleroo* when it is followed by the dative case in New Testament Greek carries the idea of "control" or "means" rather than "content." In other words, we will not get any more of the Holy Spirit than we received on the day we were saved. The question is, will He get more of us! Therefore, everything in life that pertains to the household of the Christian family, including the master-slave relationship, should be governed by the control and guidance of the Holy Spirit. Such control leads to racial and class harmony.

As we can see, the language event hermeneutic is a very valuable tool for bringing the Scriptures to life because it uses life as its interpretive key. However, what about all those events and doctrines in the Bible that are alien to our life experience, as well as the types of literary genre to which we are not accustomed? Formal training is needed to bridge these gaps. It is in these areas that the White counterpart of the Black preacher has had a decided advantage.

Black evangelicalism seeks to take advantage of both worlds. It wants to acquire skills in the area of biblical exegesis, yet maintain the vast riches of the African-American which are rooted in our African heritage. Black clergymen need this type of exposure to biblical study, not to make us preachers, for such we already are, but to make us better preachers.

Furthermore, when an African-American walks onto the campus of a predominantly White evangelical seminary, it is not as though he brings nothing to the table. He has a plethora of knowledge about preaching and leadership that should be tapped. When African-American evangelicals and White evangelicals come together it is a win-win situation, that is, if we can remember a couple of basic principles: ". . . with humility of mind let each of you regard one another as more important than himself" (Phil. 2:3), and "Behold, how good and pleasant it is for brothers to dwell together in unity!" (Ps. 133:1).

THE CONTEXT OF BLACK PREACHING

Black preaching is set in the context of Black church worship. The American aspects of the Black church provide the format of how the liturgical aspect of the church will be formatted. Yet it is the African traditionalism which gives the Black church and its style of worship the freedom to improvise and innovate. For example, to hear "Amazing Grace" sung in a Black church is distinctively different than hearing it sung in White churches. I doubt seriously if John Newton would have ever envisioned that particular version.

There are three primary sources that Henry Mitchell recognized as essential to the formulation of the distinct African-American style of worship. Mitchell says,

> The testimony of the ex-slaves includes and/or implies three written American sources of folk theology in addition to their frequent mention of the crucial and widely familiar "spirituals." The first source is their common quotation of biblical texts popular among slaves, a theological index at least as important as the spiritual songs, if not more so. A second source emerges in occasionally quoted and highly popular White hymns, which also reveal beliefs they held dear and appropriated. . . . Then thirdly, there are Black restatements of doctrines of White origin which are highly significant.[6]

The role of music has always had a significant place in the worship of Africans and their descendants. Remember that much of African Traditional Religion was transferred through hymns and songs which resembled the Psalms of the Old Testament. The music in the Black church then takes on the form of the Word of God as it is sung. This notion and appreciation for the genre of song is rooted deep within the core of the African heart. Because the orientation toward the ministry of music is set in this vein, the music of the Black church has had a profound impact on the American culture at large. This is why the Negro spiritual has become such a significant part of American life.

In many cases, the music in the Black church is a way of drawing people into the church. Thus a partnership is formed between the pulpit and the choir. The product of this partnership is a unique form of evangelism. Few Black preachers allow their sermons to conclude without giving a call to accept Christ as Lord and Savior. Concomitant with his call to discipleship, the choir proclaims the same truth about God's grace, power, and mercy which softens the heart of the sinner and brings him up front before all the church to make his/her confession of trusting Christ for salvation.

It was noted during slavery how much the slaves dressed in their best whenever they came to church. This custom was a carry-over from Africa. The worship of God was a celebration. It was a festive event celebrating life which God both supplied and reigned over. For the slave, the worship service was the only time that he was free. The goodness of God could be celebrated without obstruction. For the slave, worship was his reaffirmation of hope. This aspect of celebrating God in worship is still visible in the mainline Black church.

Although slavery has ended, the theme of freedom remains. Where there is hope for freedom, there is much joy and exuberance.

A natural application of the principle of Black freedom is to be found in the music of Black worship. If the Holy Spirit is assumed to take over the specifics of a prayer or a sermon, why not the details of a musical rendition also? Thus Black worship frowns on the meticulous adherence to the printed melodic line.[7]

This mode of celebrative worship is quite biblical. Consider the tenor of Psalm 92 titled, "A Song for the Sabbath day."

It is good to give thanks to the Lord, and to sing praises to Thy name, O Most High; To declare Thy loving-kindness in the morning, and Thy faithfulness by night, with the ten-stringed lute, and with the harp; with resounding music upon the lyre. For Thou, O Lord, hast made me glad by what Thou hast done.

The scenario of the Jews of the Old Testament has its affinities with the plight of the African-American. Therefore, it is not unreasonable to find similarities in their respective styles of worship. Exuberance and glee should not be banned from the worship of God. Sacredness does not necessarily imply that we have to be solemn and silent. Of course, there are occasions when silence is appropriate, but when the African-American considers the care and protection God supplies, especially in light of his socio-economic plight, it is difficult not to be expressive.

It is perhaps the same principle that is at work in the parable that Christ tells in Luke 7:41-42. The scene which was the impetus for the parable is the episode where the Lord dined at the house of Simon the Pharisee. At the dinner was a woman whom the Bible refers to as a "sinner" who brought a vial of perfume in order to anoint Jesus' feet. As she knelt at His feet, "she began to wet His feet with her tears, and kept wiping them with the hair of her head, and kissing His feet, and anointing them with the perfume" (7:38).

It seems that Simon the Pharisee found this type of appreciation given to Jesus to be excessive and improper. Furthermore, she was a social outcast, "a sinner." Jesus addressed Simon's insensitivity with a parable. "A certain moneylender had two debtors: one owed five hundred denarii, and the other fifty. When they were unable to repay, he graciously forgave them both. Which of them therefore will love him more?" Simon then answered, "I suppose the one whom he forgave more." To which Jesus replied, "You have judged correctly."

When we observe the worship style of Black people, we observe a people who owe much in thankfulness to God. The mode of worship will seem abnormal, just as the woman's actions toward Jesus appeared to be odd. But the so-called abnormality is in proportion to the degree of thankfulness due to the God who has granted forgiveness and a promise of a better life. Therefore, it would be abnormal for Black worship if we did not render to God our whole selves for the sake of worship. It is this tenet that governs the manner of worship in the Black church.

THE CONTEMPORARY STATUS OF THE BLACK PREACHER

Today the Black preacher remains atop the pinnacle of Black community leadership, although it is not as high a pinnacle as in days gone by. Since the Black church is still the most dominant institution in Black America, and since the Black preacher is still its primary leader, he holds the primary role as divine representative and cultural influencer.

The reasons for a more diminished role of the Black preacher are numerous. First, the Black community ministers to a more diversified and stratified clientele. In slavery, all were slaves or severely limited by the social limitations of slavery. Not so since the civil rights impact. With diversity of opportunity has come diversity of expertise. Thus, all do not now automatically look to the Black preacher for leadership. Because there has been the failure on the part of many pastors to look to, learn from, and adequately utilize the variety of skills in the church, there is a generation of Blacks who do not see the church as relevant to their needs. They perceive the church as "spiritual" only, and thus unable to address the complex needs of modern society. To combat this, pastors must take more seriously the Apostle Paul's admonition to prepare the saints to do the work of the ministry (Eph. 4:11-12). Failure to use the expertise of the congregation adequately will result in an increase in disillusionment.

Another reason for the diminished role of the Black preacher is that the spiritual has taken a secondary role to the social and political in recent times. Far too many issues are fought without concern for biblical methodology, personal salvation, and theological ethics. This is one of the reasons why the success of the civil rights movement was short-lived. Even though laws were changed, hearts were not; thus, there did not exist the internal changes necessary to sustain the social and political changes that were made. Throughout Black church history, personal conversion was at the root of social conversion. This is a diminished priority today, and the progress of the Black church and the influence of the Black preacher have suffered greatly because of it.

God is not obligated to bring about social transformation that is not predicated on His standards. This requires that preachers hold Black organizations accountable for the methods they use to bring about Black liberation. Far too many social, political, and economic programs automatically expect and demand Black church endorsement and participation simply predicated on their supposed representation of the Black community. These programs want to set the agenda for the church's participation rather than having the church, based on biblical criteria, establish the agenda. This uncritical support by the church is detrimental. If the Black preacher is to reexperience his greatness, he must return to the authority of the Bible.

A third reason for the diminished role of the Black preacher today is the absence of accountability which has led to increased scandals. Such scandals have led to a decrease in respect for the clergy in general. Historically, the Black church demanded that its clergy be accountable for their lifestyles. Immorality, drunkenness, carousing, and stealing were grounds for quick and decisive action and discipline regardless of whether it occurred in the pulpit or the pew. It is imperative that Black clergy develop and adhere to some system of accountability in order to regain the credibility that is necessary for leadership to be respected and followed. The Black preacher must take much more seriously the call to holiness and personal righteousness if he is to experience divine assistance in his attempts to help transform society.

A fourth reason for the diminished role of the clergy is the new dependent posture of the Black community in general and the Black church in particular. In slavery, the Black community had to look within itself for meaning, hope, direction, and stability. It drew exclusively from the resources provided by God in order to find the freedom it knew God had granted it. The preacher was the focal point of the community because it could not look outside itself for meaningful leadership. This allowed the Black church to rise as a truly independent institution that determined its own direction and destiny under God and through the direction of the Black preacher.

This is tragically not the case today. The Black community has become, to a large degree, a dependent community. It is so dependent on government and entitlement programs for its existence that the church is perceived in many quarters merely as a vehicle to help channel those programs to the community. Thus, if the government does not do it, it does not get done. In slavery, however, no such dependency existed because no such dependency was available. The Black preacher oversaw a comprehensive institution that clothed the naked, fed the hungry, established businesses, and took care of its orphans. Today those responsibilities have been handed over to the state. Why look to the preacher and the church when you can look to Uncle Sam?

Despite the areas of needed improvement, the Black preacher still holds the key to the success or failure of the Black community's vision of liberation. Just as he provided comprehensive, qualitative leadership through the most tumultuous times Black people have ever faced, he is still poised to accomplish that again as he uses the Bible as his primary manual for freedom. Failure to seize the moment, however, will turn the diminished pinnacle into a disastrous precipice both for himself and the Black community.

NOTES—CHAPTER 5

[1] Quoted by H. Beecher Hicks, Jr. in his book *Images of the Black Preacher* (Valley Forge, PA.: Judson Press, 1977), p. 25 is Jackson W. Carroll, "Images of Ministry: Some Correlates and Consequences" (Paper delivered at Emory University, Atlanta, Georgia).

[2] Henry H. Mitchell, *Black Preaching*, p. 65.

[3] Charles V. Hamilton, *The Black Preacher in America*, p. 102.

[4] Ibid., pp. 32-36. Three of the four cultural transformations are identified.

[5] Richard Soulen, "Black Worship and Hermeneutic," *Christian Century*, 87 (June 1970), pp. 169-70.

[6] Henry H. Mitchell, *Black Belief*, p. 97.

[7] Ibid.

Chapter 6

The Rise of Black Evangelicalism

*B*y the term "Black Evangelicalism," we refer to that movement among Christians of African-American descent which seeks to harmoniously systematize and integrate the reality of the Black experience with the strengths of a conservative approach to the Bible, theology, and ministry. In order to understand this recent phenomenon and its implications for American Christianity in general and the Black church in particular, we must understand the confluence of themes that lead to this distinctive movement within the Black church.

There are three themes in particular that provide the historical, theological, and social backdrop to the development of this ecclesiastical phenomenon. First of all, there is the conservative nature of the Black church. Secondly, there is the theological contradiction of the White church. Finally, there is the influence of the Black revolution and its resultant religious consequences. When these themes are woven together, they become the basis of a formal movement that could unite the strengths of Black and White Christians for a wholistic approach to cultural impact.

THE CONSERVATIVE NATURE OF THE BLACK CHURCH

The Black church has historically been evangelical long before the term "evangelical" was coined by Harold John Ockenga.[1] If doctrinal beliefs are the fundamental criteria for what is "evangelical" and what is not, then we would have to say that, historically, the Black church has been evangelical because it has always held to the historic Protestant Christian doctrine.

The Evangelical Theological Dictionary defines evangelicalism as "The movement in modern Christianity, transcending denominational and confessional boundaries, that emphasizes conformity to the basic tenets of the faith and a missionary outreach of compassion and urgency."[2] Theologically, there is stress on the sovereignty of God, the transcendent, personal, and infinite Being who created and rules over heaven and earth. Furthermore, evangelicals regard Scripture as the divinely inspired record of God's revelation and the infallible, authoritative guide for faith and practice. In addition, the person and work of Christ as the perfect God-man who came to earth as God's means of providing salvation are seen as the center of the evangelical Christian message.

Given the above generally accepted criteria, we cannot speak of evangelicalism and in the process exclude the historical Black church. In fact, the Black church was founded and flourished in a conservative biblical tradition. Historically, this has been true without regard to denominational affiliation.

One of the reasons why the evangelical tradition of the Black church has not been taken seriously by the broader evangelical community is because its theological expression has taken the form of oral genre rather than a literary tradition resulting in textbooks and formal theological statements. This tendency to employ and prefer an oral form of communication springs from the ancestral practices of the African forefathers. Black preaching and the spirituals validated the reality of evangelical doctrine even though the doctrinal formulas were not systematically expressed.[3]

In the early Black church, there was no tendency toward systemization. That is, there were no systematic theologies produced by Blacks. The Black church employed the use of oratory genres conducive to producing a living expression of their theology. Therefore, their doctrines walked with them. Doctrinal formulae were not reduced to writing. Thus, it was difficult to estrange the biblically informed philosophy of life of the Black member and that of his practice.

Given this tendency toward oral expression, we need only to listen to what was preached and prayed.[4] When I examined the narratives of Negro history and even the antebellum homilies, it was clear that the "Negro" Christian believed the right things about God, the right things about Christ, and the right things about the Spirit. He did not utilize the word "omnipotent"; he simply said, "there's nothing God can't do." The witness of Luke 1:37, "For nothing will be impossible with God," was for him an all-sufficient statement and was fully credible because Scripture attested it. The "Negro" Christian did not talk about the infinity of God, but he knew "God was so high you couldn't get over Him, so low you couldn't get under Him, and so wide you couldn't go around Him," which meant precisely the same thing. He spoke biblical truth in different terminology, but the nature of his theology was very evangelical.

Moreover, since the Black church could not participate in the mainstream of American Christianity, it never participated in the theological controversies that developed in the White Christian community. Blacks were not allowed to attend White schools; as a consequence, they were alienated from the controversies of the day and never really had the opportunity to become liberal. In the early 1900s, for instance, controversies emerged in higher theological educational institutions over the new liberalism which denied the virgin birth and the inspiration of Scripture.[5] These controversies did not enter into the sphere of Black religion because Blacks were denied access to the forums and academic areas where such matters were discussed and debated. Neither of these things would have been of any major concern for Blacks.

For Black Christians caught in a web of oppression and injustice, a much more beneficial enterprise was to formulate a theology of existence and liberation. Other issues were moot and thus deserved a mute response, especially since the formal categories of conservative theology were embedded in the Black community's world view.

The theologian for the Black church was the Black preacher. Everything that was pertinent to know about God was articulated in Scripture which was his lone authority. If he did not believe his Bible, he could never ascend to the pulpit of the Black church. An example of how the Black preacher thought about theology was recently provided by a Dallas Theological Seminary student from Burma. This student was having a difficult time with the introduction to theology (Prolegomena). It was not that the subject matter was too complex for him, but the nature of the study seemed somehow awkward. The class was studying apologetics, specifically the arguments for the existence of God. After the class he remarked, "About such things, I fail to see the necessity to discourse. Where I am from we never question, much less debate, the existence of God."

This was the ideological framework of the Black preacher as well. The Bible states in Genesis 1:1, "In the beginning God. . . ." Since the Scripture from its very inception assumed the existence of God, all discussion involving such vain patterns of thought would be viewed as an utter misuse of time for senselessness, and it also would draw much criticism and mockery.

The fact that little educational opportunity was available to the Black community also kept liberal thought from infiltrating the Black church. In other words, since the enslaved Black church had limited access to formal academic training, it never participated in the technical theological debates of the broader community. The Black community was content to listen to the preacher and measure his credibility against what the Bible said and whether his lifestyle validated his message. The preacher had to be conservative in order to be the preacher. Thus, the Black church was sheltered from becoming liberal.[6] On the other hand, the White church began gravitating toward liberalism and needed to fight to retain its conservative posture.

THE THEOLOGICAL CONTRADICTION OF THE WHITE CHURCH

While the Black church has historically been an evangelical institution, Black evangelicalism has become a growing and distinct movement within the Black church since World War II. As nineteenth-century liberal German rationalism and scholasticism began to infect the White churches and their institutions early in the twentieth century, there was a concerted effort by White fundamentalists to fight back against this theological intrusion into American conservative theology. This antiliberalism movement gave rise to alternative religious institutions culminating in the Bible College movement[7] which sought to train a new generation of youth in historical conservative theology and prepare them to convert the culture back to God.

As American universities and seminaries became more and more liberal, however, they simultaneously became more and more open racially. Liberal schools began leading the way in providing religious education to Blacks. Conservative schools, on the other hand, were very slow to open their doors to Blacks.[8] In order to salve their consciences for maintaining the color line while providing some formal evangelical training to Black people, Bible colleges developed separate but equal (most times unequal) evening training programs for Blacks, called "Institutes."

Black Christians exposed to these conservative training centers and the ministries that they spawned, such as Youth for Christ, Campus Crusade for Christ, the Navigators, and Young Life, developed a social/theological dialectical tension. On the one hand, Black Christians were, for the first time, being significantly exposed to a systematic approach to learning and understanding the spiritual truths which they had always believed. On the other hand, they were also faced with the reality and social implications of the alienation of their race.

The same group of people who advocated "the unity of the body" from Ephesians 4:4-6 were also ardent practitioners of racial segregation. The implicit message was, "Let's win their souls, but not deal with them as people." As the graduates of these institutions trekked to the extremities of the earth to fulfill the Great Commission of Matthew 28:19-20 and Acts 1:8, they successfully overlooked the Jerusalem, Judea, and Samaria in their own backyard here in the Americas. As for the Black graduates, most mission societies would not receive them as candidates, qualified or not.

Somehow, the conservative White Christian did not actualize the truth of Ephesians 2:14-15, that Christ has become the peace of all men who are members of His body, the church. White evangelical theologians understood well the theology of Ephesians 4, but functioned as though these instructions had been given by Immanuel Kant[9] and not the Apostle Paul through the agency of the Holy Spirit. It became increasingly apparent that while Blacks could learn systematic formula for understanding the Bible and theology in these institutions, they could only find meaningful relationships and self-identity there in a limited way.

Some Black evangelicals, caught in a Christianity versus culture identity crisis, made the mistake of viewing and analyzing their own history, culture, and church experience through the lens of the White theological perspective. This was a disaster, as many joined Whites in assessing Black religion as being "that ignorant, uneducated, over-emotional group of people," resulting in an alienation from the very community that birthed them and that needed their new expertise. This left many Black evangelicals caught in a matrix of confusion since they had been taught to be biblical before being cultural.

It became evident to Black Christians that they were never going to be fully accepted in the broader White evangelical structure. If Black Christians were going to prioritize the evangelization of Black America successfully and maintain their cultural distinctives, they were going to have to unite for the purpose of fellowship and ministry. So, in 1963 a group of Black leaders caucused together and formed the National Negro Evangelical Association[10] (NNEA), the first distinctively Black evangelical organization.

Although a distinctive movement, the NNEA did not abandon its denominational affiliations for a number of obvious reasons. Since the evangelical burden was primarily designed to impact Black Americans, Black evangelicals needed to be where those Black people were, the Black church. Since all the institutions in the Black communities intersect with the Black church and since all Black leadership intersects with the Black church, it was imperative that Black evangelicals not lose that relationship. Finally, maintaining a relationship with the Black church was crucial because of the common participation in the Black experience and the need to maintain the transference of Black culture from an evangelical perspective.

The NNEA, which later was renamed the National Black Evangelical Association, became the rallying point and primary information center for Black evangelical outreach, leadership exposure, fellowship, and theological debate. It would also serve as the Black evangelical community's representative arm to the White evangelical community.

As a result of its influence, many other leaders and organizations are helping to fulfill that role.

Currently, Black evangelicals simultaneously minister in three spheres of Christian service. First, we serve in White church and para-church ministries that have some level of ministry outreach to the Black community. Additionally, we serve in independent churches that no longer identify intimately with the mainline Black church denominational structure. Finally, we minister in mainline Black churches and their denominational church structure. Regardless of the sphere of ministry, the unifying factor is our burden for the spiritual state of Black America, the need for Black and White reconciliation, and commitment to the authority of the Scripture.

THE INFLUENCE OF THE BLACK REVOLUTION

With the rise of the Negro Revolution,[11] which later became known as the Black Revolution, a community-wide effort developed to comprehensively change the social-political situation in America. Even though such efforts had been the goal of the Black community throughout its history, for the first time a national movement led by Blacks developed to change the legal and political structures that help perpetuate American racism.

Again, the Black church was called upon to provide leadership and cohesiveness to the movement which became a clarion call for Black Power.[12] Out of the womb of the Black church emerged the Rev. Dr. Martin Luther King, Jr., who became the leader, spokesperson, and torchbearer for this latest call for freedom.

It was during this period that "Negroes," who were previously "colored," became "Black." That is, the Black community no longer viewed itself in terms of the broader White definitions, but now sought to define itself. This new self-consciousness gave rise to everything from new hair styles and dress to a renewed interest and examination of African history and culture. Black people were now going to determine for themselves who they were and where they were going.

The new Black Revolution began to need theological interpretation to address the questions that were arising from its impact on American society. Questions such as, "What does it mean to be Black and Christian?," and "What did Christ have to say about the hypocrisy of the White religionists who simultaneously spoke of Christianity while maintaining racist structures?" Also, what was Christ saying about the violence that had become a part of the Black effort for freedom?

These questions and others like them gave rise to the first attempt in Black history to develop a systematic theology of Black liberation. This system became known as Black Theology. Leading in the development of this new theology was James Cone.[13] Cone, leaning heavily on liberal theology and theologians, coupled with an analysis of the Black experience in America, concluded that there could be no true understanding of God, the Bible, and Christianity apart from the liberation motif.

Black evangelicals found themselves caught between two worlds. On the one hand, they held tenaciously to a conservative approach to theology which gave them linkage to the White evangelical world, yet they also had to respond to the call for Black liberation which brought them into conflict with their White mentors. On the other hand, Black evangelicals supported the clarion call for justice, yet disagreed with many of Black Theology's conclusions that were undergirding that call. This forced Black evangelicals to further become a distinctive emphasis within the Black church as well as within the broader American evangelical church.

THE CONCERNS OF BLACK EVANGELICALISM

Black Evangelicalism was born and has developed out of a number of concerns relative to both the Black and White church in America. Realizing that both groups have major strengths and weaknesses, Black evangelicals seek to extract and build simultaneously on the strengths of both while seeking also to address the weaknesses of both.

One of the major concerns of Black Evangelicalism is the evangelization of the Black community in America. This concern has been born out of the fact that the White church has had little interest in missions across the street in its own Black Samaria. Having been exposed to the quality tools that have been developed to accomplish effective "soul winning," Black evangelicals have taken this mission upon themselves. The distinction of Black evangelicals from the Black church in general is the aggressive nature of this personal evangelism in light of the concern that the social and political movements of the day, while valid, are missing this eternal aspect of God's agenda.

A second concern, tied somewhat to the first, is regarding the need for spiritual renewal in the Black church. The burden developed that certain traditions were getting in the way of effective ministry. Many Black evangelicals (including this writer) feel that the Bible and biblical ministry has been taking a back seat to man-made traditions. It is the concern of this group of Black evangelicals that church programs be evaluated by two primary criteria: is it biblical and does it work?

While we recognize that many "old time ways" are important for maintaining cultural continuity and spiritual vitality, we also recognize that this generation needs ministry that is contemporaneous to its social, educational, attitudinal, psychological, marital, parental, and career needs and aspirations. Thus, the emphasis of Black evangelicals is on the need for a multi-staff approach to ministry, with the pastor leading the way, so that the multi-faceted needs of the people can be met in a timely and effective manner.

Intricately tied into the ministry emphasis of Black evangelicalism is the clarion call for more teaching. While it is readily admitted that the Black pastor has constantly maintained the celebrative aspects of worship, there is a greater need for training Black people in the more didactic aspects of Scripture if we are going to be sufficiently equipped to function in our contemporary society. There is a particular emphasis here on expository preaching, which is the logical, progressive explanation of a passage of Scripture in its context so the audience can understand its meaning and learn how to apply it to their lives. This is a particular concern given the educational advancements the Black community has undergone. Such exposition, however, must never lose sight of the great biblically based sermonic and worship history and motif of the Black church.

A further concern of Black Evangelicalism is racial reconciliation. While this has always been a desire of the Black church throughout its history, Black evangelicals have taken an aggressive posture to implement this process. Since many of these evangelical leaders regularly interface with the White evangelical church, we are in a unique position to help facilitate the process (often having to overcome great opposition from the White community to do so). The effects of these efforts have resulted in many cooperative ministry outreaches.

Finally, Black Evangelicalism places a major emphasis on discipleship as opposed to simply church membership. That is, processes are being intentionally developed to help Christians bring every area of their lives under the lordship of Jesus Christ. This is seen in the augmenting of Sunday worship services with church and home Bible studies, fellowship groups, one-on-one partnerships, and the use of specially designed discipleship curriculum.

Closely related to this discipleship emphasis is the need to address sinful lifestyles. Black evangelicals emphasize the need for church discipline for unrepentant church members, the removal of unqualified leaders, and the restoration of those who repent.

This fast growing group within the Black church has had to be careful not to throw out the cultural baby with the errant theological bath water, for while the emphasis is thoroughly biblical, we have sometimes been guilty of rejecting legitimate aspects of Black tradition and worship that should and must be maintained.

This movement is in a most unique position to serve in a long line of strategic "links" to help strengthen the ministry of the Black church while simultaneously educating the White church to the comprehensive cultural impact of the gospel. The enslaved Black church married the best of African religion and culture with the Christian faith to forge out a unique imprint on the American religious scene. In the same way, Black Evangelicalism seeks to facilitate the fusion of the best of the Black church and the best of the White church to hew out what could very well be the strongest, unifying, comprehensive, contemporary expression of biblical Christianity ever.

THE CONTRIBUTIONS OF BLACK EVANGELICALISM

The presence of a distinctive, Black evangelical emphasis which adheres to the major theological tenets of biblical Christianity, while at the same time maintaining a concern for the oppressed and the social realities of the Black experience, provides the Christian church with a number of contributions that can enhance the overall well-being of Christianity in America.

First of all, Black evangelicals provide the White church with a clearer understanding of the major biblical themes of justice and liberation, using language and biblical categories to which the White church can relate. Because Black evangelicals have the same conservative view of the authority of Scripture as White evangelicals, we are in a unique position to communicate a biblical emphasis that has been sorely neglected. The effect of this has already been demonstrated in the major changes that have occurred in the White evangelical structure, such as: the development of urban outreaches, increases in Black religious study curricula, greater representation in the mainstream of American evangelicalism, and a heightened recognition of African-American contribution to the overall development of Christianity in America.

Increasingly, concerted efforts are being made to address the ethical issues of our day and not merely the epistemological ones. The Black evangelical presence has sensitized many in the White evangelical world to confront racism as sin and not simply as culturally acceptable behavior. Black evangelicalism has helped to broaden significantly the definition of evangelicalism to include the issues of social justice.

Secondly, Black evangelism provides the Black church with a desperately needed systematic approach to the Bible and theology. While it was acceptable not to have such a systematic approach in times past, that is not the case today. As the Black community has become exposed increasingly to education, it has also increased in its liberal influence. As more and more trained clergy take their place behind the pulpits of Black churches, there is a need for a clearly articulated biblical theology for the Black experience so that the historical, evangelical posture of the Black church can be maintained in a contemporary way.

Also, because Black evangelicals have had extensive exposure to some of the strengths of the established, White institutional church structure, we have gained various expertise which are critical for the Black church to incorporate if it is going to be effective in its ministry to this contemporary generation. Such expertise includes everything from multi-staffed ministries to fund-raising processes to the development of para-church ministries that support the local church.[14]

Finally, and of greatest importance, is the unique opportunity Black evangelicals have to promote unity between the Black and White church. Because Black evangelicals have lived on both sides of the American ecclesiastical divide, we are uniquely positioned to mediate the beginning of a new era of racial harmony and cooperation among Christians who are culturally different, yet spiritually one.

NOTES—CHAPTER 6

[1]Harold John Ockenga coined the phrase "new evangelicalism" in 1948 to refer to progressive fundamentalism with a social message. The evangelical movement was born out of a need to purge fundamentalism of its sectarian, combative, anti-intellectual and anti-cultural traits. Ockenga became the organizational leader of the movement. He planned and promoted the National Association of Evangelicals, serving as its president from 1942-44. He was also instrumental in the founding of Fuller Theological Seminary, which became one of the leading scholarly institutions of the fundamentalism reformation movement.

[2]Walter Elwell, *The Evangelical Theological Dictionary*, (Grand Rapids: Baker Book House, 1989), p. 379.

[3]See James H. Cone, *The Spirituals and the Blues*, for a summary of the relationship of music to the theology of the Black church.

[4]See Harold Carter's, *The Prayer Tradition of Black People*.

[5]Debate raged because of the propositions of the German scholar Rudolf Bultmann who contested the validity of miracle in Scripture and thus found it necessary to demythologize the Bible.

[6]Also known as modernism, this is the major shift in theological thinking that occurred in the late nineteenth century. It is an extremely explosive concept. The major thrust was to contemporize the archaisms of language and thought of the ancient word into forms and images which were more conducive to the modern world.

[7]The Bible College movement began to call for a reemphasis on the fundamentals of the faith, to counteract the growth of liberalism. Out of the Bible College movement came the Bible Institute Movement which became an auxiliary means of educating Blacks. Schools like Moody Bible Institute and Philadelphia College of the Bible developed night schools for Blacks.

[8]For example, my alma mater, Dallas Theological Seminary, would not admit Blacks until about 1968. DTS, which had long

been a bastion of conservative Christian education and a factory for producing conservative writers, thinkers, and expositors, kept the doors shut to Blacks due to the cultural climate of the day. This was true for most evangelical institutions.

[9]Immanuel Kant was a German philosopher who endorsed the enterprise of human thinking apart from the Scriptures, the Church, and the State.

[10]For a history of the NBEA, see William Bentley's, *The National Black Evangelical Association*.

[11]The Black Power movement arose on the heels of the Negro Revolution that began early in 1960. On February 1, 1960, four students from the Negro Agricultural and Technical College in Greensboro, North Carolina, were refused coffee at a local variety store because they were Negroes. In an act of rebellion, they sat at the counter until the store closed. This was the beginning of sit-ins that were to spread across the South. These protests spread because they rested on the heels of the Supreme Court decisions on voting and school desegregation and the Montgomery bus boycott under the leadership of Martin Luther King. By the summer of 1960, the status of the Negro had become a burning issue on the national conscience, and Negro preoccupation with Civil Rights had infiltrated every aspect of the community. By 1968, large demonstrations across the country began taking place to force the issues of justice and equality and to protest the violence against Negroes. The success of these sit-ins and demonstrations evidenced itself in the 1964 Civil Rights Act, which was the most far-reaching and comprehensive law in support of racial equality ever enacted by Congress. However, the "White backlash" to the Act precipitated more violence as the Ku Klux Klan protested against racial equality and injustice, and discrimination continued to increase. See John Hope Franklin, *From Slavery to Freedom*, ch. 31 and William Brink and Louis Harris, *The Negro Revolution in America*, for more detailed information.

[12]The term Black Power made its official entrance on the American scene in June 1966 with Stokely Carmichael, head of the Student Nonviolent Coordinating Committee (SNCC). It

was the call for Black people to unite and form a unified basis for demanding what was their just piece of the "American dream." It was the official call for Black self-determination and the rejection of all the racist institutions and values of American society. Black Power called for group solidarity so that as a group it could demand the emancipation of Black people from White oppression by any and all means necessary.

[13]Cone argued that there needed to be a new way of looking at theology that would emerge out of the dialectic of Black history and culture. He argues that theology had to address the question, What has the gospel to do with the Black struggle for liberation? From his position as Assistant Professor of Theology at Union Theological Seminary, he crafted three major works which were designed to begin answering that question: *Black Theology and Black Power, A Black Theology of Liberation,* and *God of the Oppressed.* Cone is known as "The Father of Black Theology."

[14]White evangelicals, for example, have provided for the spiritual development of their children from elementary school through college. As children they are covered by Child Evangelism Fellowship. As teenagers they are covered by Young Life and Youth for Christ and as college students they are covered by Campus Crusade for Christ and the Navigators. No such national tracking systems exist in Black America.

Chapter 7
The Biblical Mandate for Unity

*I*t is nothing short of tragic that the issue of the color line has been one of the major problems facing American society in the twentieth century. As W. E. B. DuBois expressed,

> I still think today as yesterday that the color line is a great problem of this century. But today I see more clearly than yesterday that back of the problem of race and color, lies a greater problem which both obscures and implements it: and that is the fact that so many civilized persons are willing to live in comfort even if the price of this is poverty, ignorance and disease of the majority of their fellowmen; that to maintain this privilege men have waged war until today war tends to become universal and continuous, and the excuse for this war continues to be color and race.[1]

Unfortunately, one of the chief manifestations of the problem of the color line is found in the Christian church, and in the evangelical church at that. Little wonder that the broader society is so anemic when it comes to unity, because the Christian church, which is supposed to be the model for societal unity, has provided so little leadership in this area. Only by discovering the cultural contributions different groups bring to the divine agenda and then blending them together for the common good can we begin to address our problem.

God not only uses individuals to contribute to His program in history but also cultures and races and people groups as well. For example, the biographical language of the Hebrews played well into the plan of God for the narrative nature of the Old Testament. This narrative emphasis was perfect for the world view of the Africans who were natural storytellers.[2] This explains the unique ability of Black preachers to weave together the thematic threads of Scripture into story form, which was an essential element for the survival of an oppressed people who had limited formal education and yet needed a comprehensive theme of liberation to lead them through the American slave maze. The story of God's deliverance of an oppressed people gave Israel a perpetual hope for freedom, and that corporate hope was adopted by the Black American church. As a result, it became the conscience of America to keep it confronted with the themes of justice, freedom, and compassion which are desperately needed if a nation is going to have a comprehensive and balanced understanding of God.

On the other hand, the language and expression of the New Testament accommodated the highly exacting philosophical context of the Greco-Roman world. The philosophical bent of the Hellenistic mind set served well the plan of God to provide a masterfully organized, doctrinal foundation for the church. The dexterity of Greek allowed the teachings of Jesus to be transmitted from the apostles to the Hellenized world of the first century in didactic formulas that would be understood, accepted, and respected. The rationale and precision of the Hellenistic culture upon which western thought is founded was precisely what the White evangelical church needed to fight against the movement of German rationalism and its influence in America through the academic institutions of the New World. The constant fight against liberalism is waged on a battlefield of words, tenets, and ideas that are dissected with precision.

The point is that God gives cultures strengths that become important for the ongoing agenda of His activity in history. The linguistic strengths mentioned above are reflected in the strengths of both the Black and White churches and are important to the program of God. On the one hand, the Black preacher has served as a model and foundation for the greatest preaching and oratorical presentation of Christian social themes America has ever seen because of his ability "to tell the story."[3] However, the most powerful literary defenses and theological centers for promulgation of the Christian faith ever developed have been provided by the White church's propensity towards didactic defense. Thus, both the Black and White churches bring something to the table to be jointly used for the promotion of the Christian faith.

Cultures, then, bring strengths that contribute to the plan of God. They are thus free to express themselves until and unless they begin to impede rather than support the program of God.

THE MEANING OF UNITY

Why has there been so little progress in race relations in American culture in general and American Christianity in particular? First of all, there is the problem of definition. Unity is not equal to sameness. Just as a husband and wife can become one, even though there are obvious physical, temperamental, and personality differences, cultures and races can be one without being the same. What then is the essence of that oneness? In order to have unity, there must be oneness of purpose. That is, both parties must be willing to move forward in a central direction for the common good of all involved. The moment a husband or wife establishes a private agenda or purpose that does not involve the overall good of the home, the marriage is in trouble. In the same way, cultures and races are in trouble that do not have a unified purpose.

The Black community has its agenda and the White community has its agenda. The problem is that there is no sufficiently overarching agenda that transcends both, a-round which our private agendas can rally. However, this need not be the case.

An illustration of what I mean was demonstrated when the Persian Gulf War broke out in 1991. Conflict between the races took a back seat to the war. Why? Because there was a bigger agenda on the table, namely Saddam Hussein and the Iraqi army. The fact that there was a threat to Black and White soldiers equally, since both were American citizens, caused people to rally around a common purpose. The issue during this brief war was not the color, culture, or race of the persons fighting next to each other. The only important issue was whether the soldiers next to each other were all shooting in the same direction at the same enemy.

When faced with a common enemy that involves a common threat, a common passion is automatically ignited which results in a unity of purpose. The problem emerges, however, when the threat dissipates. The result is all too often a return to the cultural posture that existed prior to the conflict. Thus, churches and Christians could pray together for peace and protection during the Middle East conflict, but hardly be willing to speak to each other after the conflict.

The Black and White churches, then, need to adopt a joint agenda of purpose that reflects and incorporates both of our concerns, while at the same time being broader than our individual concerns.

A perfect illustration of such a scenario is the abortion debate. The White evangelical church is heavily Republican because of its belief that the Republican Party best reflects the concerns of Christians for the need for a moral awakening in our country. Because a large segment of the Republican Party is antiabortion, the watershed issue of the moral agenda, the White evangelical church has made the abortion debate the center of its concern.

On the other hand, the Black church has, in recent history, given its dominant allegiance to the Democratic Party because of its belief that the Democratic Party is more sensitive to the questions of social justice, racial equality, and the plight of the poor. The abortion question, while legitimate, is simply not that high on the list of concerns of the Black church because of the nature of its history of oppression in America. The Black church's heart cry is primarily for the comprehensive well-being of the babies born in the world (specifically in the area of employment, housing, medical care, equal access, and education), rather than the safety of the fetus in the womb.

What is the solution? Simply, it is to establish an agenda of purpose that includes both issues since both issues are legitimate and have ample biblical support; in other words, unify around a perspective that encompasses a "whole life" agenda rather than simply a "term life" agenda. Leaders from both sides should establish a purpose that goes from cradle to grave and womb to tomb. Such an approach would unify the church around a central theme that both sides can agree on, while at the same time allowing each side to focus on the area of its primary concern. There would not be sameness, but there would be oneness, and that is what biblical unity is all about.

The bonus to all of this would be that the broader culture would see the unity of the church as it works across racial lines for our common agendas, resulting in the fulfillment of Jesus' words, "By this all men will know that you are My disciples if you have love for one another (John 13:35). What greater love can we show for one another than by working together to seek the comprehensive welfare of the members of God's family first, and then extending that concern to the culture at large?

THE LIMITATIONS OF CULTURE

A major obstacle to overcome in establishing biblically-based unity is the question of who's in charge: the Bible or one's culture? One of the major hindrances to biblical unity is the authority given to cultural diversity. For example, Black Christians will often so amalgamate Black culture with their faith that they frequently fail to make the necessary distinction between the two. Many times White racism is blamed for what really is Black irresponsibility, for which we are not willing to take responsibility (i.e., teenage pregnancy, Black on Black crimes, absentee fathers). We far too often appeal to White oppression to excuse Black ineptness as though we are such a weak, powerless, ungifted people that we can only function to the degree others allow us.

Conversely, Whites will leave the Bible when it is culturally convenient to do so in order to protect their traditions. This is seen most clearly in the sacred cow of interracial dating and marriage. When the issue comes up, it is amazing how quickly the argument of culture comes up. Questions like, "What about the kids?" and "What will the relatives think?" come to the surface much quicker than what the Bible says. To be sure, some very legitimate questions should be raised as to whether all the issues have been thought through and properly filtered before such a serious step is taken; however, more often than not, these individuals fail to come clean and acknowledge that God has nothing to say against such marriages between two Christians.

The problem with both of these perspectives is the failure to recognize biblical authority when it clashes with cultural or racial presuppositions and practices. This problem is in no way unique to the Black-White racial landscape, for it is equally evident in the world of the New Testament. For instance, Galatians 2 records one such incident. This particular illustration is graphic because it involved apostolic leadership, the highest authorities in the first century church. Peter, "the stone," was a committed Jew. He loved his people and carried a deep burden for their salvation. God, however, expanded his horizon by giving him the experience of seeing that the very same work God was doing among Jews was also repeated among the Gentiles (Acts 10--11). Peter accepted that revelation and seemed to have understood it.

However, the Apostle Paul recorded a confrontation with Peter that revealed old prejudices do not die easily. Peter was enjoying fellowship with Gentile Christians. During this time of cross-cultural intermingling, in walked Jewish Christians who had not yet come to grips with their anti-Gentile racism, putting Peter on the spot. He was faced with the choice of relinquishing his fellowship with the Gentile Christians in order to satisfy the desires of his cultural Christian brothers or standing for the truth of the equality of Gentiles with Jews in the body of Christ. Peter miserably failed the test. In deference to the cultural pressure of his own race, he discredited the message of the gospel which God had so graphically conveyed to him in the home of Cornelius. He left the Gentiles in order not to offend the Jews.

There was only one problem; Paul saw it. When Paul, who was equally committed to his Jewish history, culture, and people, saw Peter's non-Christian action, he publicly condemned it because Peter's action was not "straight forward about the truth of the gospel" (Gal. 2:14). The key point is "truth." There was an objective standard that transcended Peter's cultural commitment, and that was the criteria by which he was judged. The fact that even an apostle could not get away with such action is very instructional. It means that no one is excused for placing culture above Christ or race above righteousness. God's standard must reign supreme, and cultural preferences are to be denounced publicly when there is a failure to submit to God's standard.

It is high time the church allows the Scripture, and only the Scripture, to be the final authority by which to judge racial relationships.

THE PRICE TAG OF UNITY

Another problem that must be addressed is the cost of unity. Unity is very expensive. Just as a husband and wife must give up a lot to gain the oneness that marriage offers, so also must races be willing to pay the price to experience biblical unity. One of the losses both sides must be willing to experience is the rejection of friends and relatives, whether Christians or non-Christians, who are not willing to accept the thesis that spiritual family relationships transcend physical, cultural, and racial relationships. This is what Jesus meant when He said, "Whoever does the will of My Father who is in heaven, he is My brother and sister and mother" (Matt. 12:50). The cost is particularly expensive to local churches who begin opening their doors to people who are viewed by many as socially unacceptable, even though they have been made acceptable to the Father by the blood of Christ.

In order to prepare for God's unity call, pastors are going to have to begin preaching the whole counsel of God. We are going to have to stop skipping James' condemnation of class distinction in the church (James 2:1-13). We are going to have to explain to our congregations the racial implications of the middle wall of partition being broken down (Eph. 2:11-18) in terms that are meaningful and applicable to the contemporary Black-White debate. We are going to have to stop ignoring Christ's teaching on the responsibility of people to tangibly demonstrate our love for our neighbor even if our neighbor is from a different culture (Luke 10:30-37).

Important as preaching is, however, it is not enough. The church must then follow up with practical opportunities for bridging the cultural divide. This includes developing a relationship with a pastor and church from another culture and starting a joint fellowship. A joint worship service is a good starting point, but that is not enough. We must then get groups within the church to begin ministering side by side. Nothing will bond people more than working together, particularly in doing works of charity.

Finally, and perhaps most costly of all, there must be the willingness to hold people accountable for refusing to cooperate with the bridge-building efforts of the church. Racism cannot just be allowed to fester without public and personal condemnation. It should be clear what the church will and will not allow. What should not be allowed is the subjection of brothers and sisters who are different to racial slurs and public rejection in the church. There is no more time for us to sit by passively and wait for people to change. People must be led into change, and that cannot be done without the knowledge that we will be held accountable for how we treat the other members of God's family.

Only if all sides are willing to take this stand will the effort be worth the risk. For one side to pay the price without equal commitment from the other is to create only more mistrust and division. However, when both sides take a strong biblical stand, the support systems will be there to withstand the opposition that will naturally come from taking such a stand for righteousness.

A LESSON IN UNITY FROM JESUS

One of the most informative and poignant teachings regarding culture, truth, and unity is in the story of Jesus' encounter with the woman of Samaria that is recorded in John 4. In this story Jesus clearly demonstrates that cultural validity is determined by its relationship to spiritual truth and promotion of Christian unity.

In 722 B.C., the Jews living in the Northern Kingdom were taken captive by the Assyrians. Some were deported to Assyria while other Assyrians were imported into the Northern Kingdom. The Jews who remained held fast to their true worship of God despite the introduction of Assyrian cults. However, there was intermarriage which destroyed the purity of the race and gave birth to a new race of people called Samaritans.

During the Persian period, the Jews were allowed to return to Jerusalem to rebuild the Temple and the walls. This attempt was resisted by the Samaritans who were now a mixed breed (Assyrians and Israelites). The Jews desired to maintain the purity of the Jewish race and thus would not allow them to participate in the rebuilding process (Neh. 2:10-6:14). A feud developed out of the incident that continued into Christ's day and served as the historical backdrop to the confrontation of Jesus with the Samaritan woman.

When Jesus traveled with His disciples through Samaria, He was not merely taking a shorter route. He was on a mission to meet needs He knew existed there. The fact that He entered Samaria made it clear that He was willing to go beyond His own culture to meet those needs, but overcoming the cultural prejudice of the Samaritans was another issue. He was willing to make the first move, but how could He get the Samaritans to give Him the chance to minister to them? The solution was to establish common ground.

In Samaria, Jesus rested at Jacob's well (John 4:6). A well offered water and shade, and it was a natural place for a hot, tired man to stop, but Jesus' reason for choosing this particular well went deeper than that. Jesus was looking for common ground. Although the Jews hated the Samaritans and the Samaritans hated the Jews, they both loved Jacob, who was the father of both groups. Therefore, Jacob was the common ground between Jesus and the woman who came to draw water. Jesus stopped at Jacob's well and built a bridge of communication by starting with what He and the woman could agree on.

Jesus had rejected the attitudes of His contemporaries in His willingness to go through Samaria from Judea to Galilee, something no good orthodox Jew would do. This is why in John 4:9 the Samaritan woman asked him, "'How is it that You being a Jew, ask me for a drink since I am a Samaritan woman?' (For Jews have no dealings with Samaritans.)"

After Jesus established common ground with the Samaritan woman, He asked her for a drink from the well. According to verse 9, the woman was dumbfounded at Jesus' request. She exclaimed, "You are a Jew and I am a Samaritan woman. How can you ask me for a drink?" She could not believe that Jesus was asking her, a woman of Samaria, to let Him use her cup. That was an act of fellowship and warm acceptance for which she was totally unprepared.

How did the woman know that Jesus was a Jew? John, the author, does not say that Jesus told her He was a Jew. Jesus was alone, so there must have been something about Him that made her know. He may have looked like a Jew. Or perhaps He had a Jewish accent or some other trait that gave a public indication of His racial and cultural heritage. Whatever it was, when Jesus Christ went through Samaria, He did not give up His own culture. He did not stop being a Jew, but He did not let His culture stop Him from meeting a spiritual need either.

Jesus did not enter into an analysis of the cultural differences between Jews and Samaritans, but rather moved to the spiritual issue of her need for forgiveness. He allowed her to hold on to her history, culture, and experience as a Samaritan. Secondly, He refused to allow culture to interfere with His higher priority of representing God's truth. When the Samaritan woman allowed her cultural background to cloud her correct understanding about God, Jesus immediately rejected her cultural commitment. He let her know in no uncertain terms that her heritage was wrong because it had caused her to draw incorrect conclusions about God, worship, truth, and sin. When her culture crossed sacred things, Christ invaded her cultural world to condemn it and let her know that her father, grandfather, and great-grandfather were all wrong. In rather direct language, Jesus said to the woman, "You worship that which you do not know" (v. 22). His point was acutely clear: whenever there is a conflict between culture and God's truth, culture must always submit to the truth of God as revealed in His Word.

That means that to refer to oneself as a Black Christian, or a White Christian, or a Mexican Christian, or a Chinese Christian is technically incorrect. In these descriptions, the word Christian becomes a noun that is modified by an adjective--Black, White, and so on. Our Christianity should never be modified by our culture; it should be just the opposite. We must see ourselves as Christian Blacks, Christian Whites, Christian Mexicans, or Christian Chinese. When we do, our cultures will be modified by the nature of our Christian commitment.

Our cultures must always be controlled by our commitment to Christ. Whenever we make the adjectives Black, White, brown, and yellow descriptive of Christians, it may mean we have changed Christianity to make it fit a cultural description. The Bible teaches the opposite--we are Christians who may happen to be Black, White, brown, or yellow. If anything changes, it is to be our cultural orientation, not our Christianity. This is so because culture, no matter how real, is not in and of itself revelatory. Cultural history and experience, while important, is not innately inspired. Therefore, Christianity must always inform, explain, and, if necessary, change our cultures--never the reverse.

Jesus not only critiqued the Samaritan culture by the truth of God's Word, but He critiqued His own culture by that same standard. When His disciples complained that He was talking with a Samaritan woman, He rejected their racism and inappropriate cultural allegiance by telling them that it was more important for Him to do the will of God than succumb to their biases (vv. 31-34). He let them know that obeying the will of God takes priority over satisfying cultural expectations. In fact, He went on to tell them that they were to stop making excuses for delaying dealing with their racial hangups (v. 35). It was harvest time and if they were going to deal with God, they were also going to have to deal with other people on God's terms and in God's time, not theirs.

Whenever a Christian acts or speaks biblically, we run the risk of being rejected. In my opinion, one of the reasons we have not experienced revival in America in recent years is that it is more popular to be an American than to be a Christian. Being an American is a privilege that gives us awesome responsibility to use our freedom to accomplish spiritual ends--not just personal ones. Others around us may not reach out cross-culturally, but that has nothing to do with whether we should reach across cultural boundaries. God expects and demands it of us.

In the Black community, there are cultural trademarks. For example, Blacks have special ways of saluting one another, shaking hands, and communicating in general. Although these marks of cultural identification and racial solidarity are acceptable, they cannot supersede spiritual identification. Therefore, White and Black Christians must learn that spiritual relationship forms the basis for true brotherhood. This is so because the bond between a Black and a White Christian is eternal, whereas the relationship between a Christian and non-Christian of the same race is temporal.

Furthermore, if Black and White Christians would maintain a tight family bond based on our relationship to Christ, there would be more unity as well as more support for one another as each of us stood against our own culture's attempt to conform us to their standards. Many believers--both Black and White--succumb to unbiblical cultural pressures because the support base created by other believers is weak. If Christians became one in purpose cross-culturally, neither Blacks nor Whites would have the strong feelings of alienation that come when we cross cultural barriers in the name of Christ.

What has all this to do with the biblical mandate for unity? Everything! It is only because Jesus was willing to press the issue on both cultures that a spiritual revival took place among the men of Sychar that led to Jesus' spending the weekend with those who only a few hours before were some of the Jewish culture's worst enemies (vv. 39-43).

It is obvious that American society has not successfully dealt with the problems of racism and prejudice. Just when it seems that major strides are being made, major reversals occur as though the racial clock is being turned back. As Christians, we have a solution, because our oneness in Christ gives us the position and power to make a statement to the world about the wonder of our faith. The very thing the world needs we have, but because we are so much like the world, the world does not know we have it. In fact, many fellow Christians do not even know we have the solution.

We must start today to work toward improving the racial situation in this country, and the place for us to begin is in the church. First and foremost, preachers and pastors must begin to address the sins of prejudice and bigotry from the pulpit. Leaders must not shy away from speaking to this issue forthrightly.

What will such a joint relationship do for our testimony to the world? Jesus makes a powerful statement in John 13:35 when He says, "By this all men will know that you are My disciples, if you have love for one another." I would have thought Jesus would have said, "By this all men will know that you are My disciples, if you have love for all people." But Jesus said that the way the world will know that we are His is through our relationship with one another in the church.

This implies two critical principles. First, Christians are to make something happen in their relationship with others that is so dynamic that the world will view it as "something worth looking at." Then, when we have the world's attention, we must do it in a way that the world will know we are relating to one another because of our relationship to Christ.

Secondly, our love for one another should be public so that unbelievers can see that Christianity is not a secret. This means our love for one another must be demonstrated outside the security of our church buildings if non-Christians are going to see it. The church needs to go public with its unity in the name of Christ. The great tragedy today is not so much that our society is still divided along racial, cultural, and ethnic lines (in reality, that is to be expected). The tragedy is rather that God's people, the church, are equally or even more deeply divided. This disunity provides Satan with his most powerful tool for crippling the influence of Christianity in our culture. That is why Jesus prayed that believers might be one in order to overcome this world (John 17:21).

The testimony of Christianity in America is racked with the embarrassment of a divided church. God does not require that all churches be integrated, but He does require that all function harmoniously as the Body of Christ without divisiveness based on race or culture. Not until the church chooses Christ over culture will the testimony and power of our witness be fully felt. Blacks and Whites must never deny our culture, history, or racial heritage unless they conflict with truth about God.

Jesus is not asking Blacks to become Whites or Whites to become Asians, but He insists that all reflect God's truth as given in Scripture. When culture does not infringe upon the Word of God, we are free to be what God has created us to be, with all the uniqueness that accompanies our cultural heritage. However, the objective truth from Scripture places limits on our cultural experience. As African-Americans continue to seek cultural freedom, we must examine every strategy offered to promote justice under the magnifying glass of Scripture. Every bit of advice given by our leaders and all definitions proposing to tell us what it means to be Black must be commensurate with divine revelation. If what we are given as cultural is not biblically acceptable, it cannot be accepted as authoritative.

Whites, too, must submit their cultural traditions to the authority of God's Word if they are going to play their part in dismantling their contribution to the racial mythology that is a dominant theme in their world view.

The bottom line then is that there must be a moral frame of reference through which both Black and White experiences are examined and judged, and the only standard that qualifies is the Bible. If we are going to experience cultural unity, then God must be true and every man a liar.

NOTES—CHAPTER 7

[1] W. E. B. DuBois, *The Souls of Black Folk*, p. XIII.

[2] Henry H. Mitchell summarizes why the African's story telling background adapted them so well to the Bible when he writes, "Blacks took the Bible seriously, and for reasons easily traceable to their African roots. In their African roots, they had known huge quantities of memorized material. Even now, the history, which is still more sung than written, is known by anybody. In one of the festivals, if the performer makes one mistake, at least 200 people will say, 'Whoa, go back.' I mentioned this because even though many of these men were illiterate, they came out of a culture where people (I Fa priests) memorized thousands of proverbs.
"In the Yoruba religion, they have sixteen Odus. Each Odu has two hundred proverbs or stories, so that some of those Yoruba priests may know about as much verbatim as we have in the whole Bible. When you go to them for leadership, guidance, or divination, these men can call it right up. This explains to a large extent the way in which Blacks adapted themselves to the Bible. The Bible was largely reflecting the kind of culture out of which they came." Henry H. Mitchell, "Black Preaching," *The Black Christian Experience*, ed. Emmanuel L. McCall, pp. 54-55.

[3] The concept of "story" refers to the historical process of God's intervention into history on behalf of the oppressed as recorded in the Bible. The Old and New Testaments are a continuous

documentation of the revelation of God in the affairs of men. The Old Testament is viewed as showing the story of salvation in the social context of the nation Israel and its deliverance from Egypt and establishment into nationhood. The New Testament is seen as the continuation of the Old Testament theme as Christ inaugurates a new age as God Himself breaking into history "to set the captive free." In keeping with this, the "Black story" comes to refer to the Black theological destination of the Black community.

Conclusion

*I*t is the quintessential contention of this author that both
the inferiority and superiority myths are just that--myths.
In fact, it is the argument of this book that the Black church
has deposited in its biblical legacy and cultural history the
clearest model of biblical Christianity in the history of
American religion. This is not because the Black church is
innately superior to the White church, but because it historically operated more in line with the comprehensive
nature of biblical revelation. The reason it did so was
because the communities' cultural-historical roots and
world view, coupled with the reality of American slavery,
forced the Black church to grapple with aspects of biblical
revelation that were unnecessary for the majority culture
to have to deal with in any comprehensive way.

Given this thesis, contemporary American Christianity
as a whole would do well to learn from the historical Black
church in order to understand in visual form the assets of
incarnational Christianity: that is, Christianity which visib-

ly displays itself in culture-wide influence, lifestyle, and social ethics. Such assets also include corporate compassion, comprehensive biblical justice, the celebrative nature of worship, wholistic ministry, and the lack of division between faith and life.

Far from being an uneducated, inept, erratic, undisciplined folk religion, the historical Black church in America was the primary proving ground for biblical Christianity. It uniquely demonstrated the relationship between love and justice. It demonstrated the nature of the church as a family and community of believers rather than simply a gathering of individualized family units. The Black church personified the relationship between faith and works and how that relationship transcends the simply personal matters of life and enters into the spheres of politics, economics, social justice, and law.

The great mosaic of the historical Black church is that there was no distinction between secular and sacred. The church demonstrated clearly that the purpose of the sacred is that it might invade the secular and transform it. It reflected and transmitted God as the epicenter of life, all of life, and it demanded that culture be called to task for any failure to recognize Him as such.

If the lessons of the historical Black church are instructional for the culture at large, then they are even more so for the Black community itself. If the church using biblical principles was able to solidify us, sustain us, protect us, promote us, house us, clothe us, feed us, employ us, and represent us during the worst of times, then how much more should we now appeal to that same biblically-based authority today! We no longer need artificial motivators to give us pride and dignity. We already have resident in our biblical God, African heritage, and Black church experience all we need to humbly stand tall. Only in God's definition of us can we find an identity that will stick because then who we are is rooted in a sovereign, immutable Being who has the last word about all things.

The only way for the Black community to advance is by going "back to the future." There is no time left for simply crying, complaining, and blaming others for the weaknesses now consuming our community. To be sure, we must recognize and use every legitimate avenue to change every expression of racism, classism, injustice, and oppression, as well as all other forms of social unrighteousness. Yet, we must never allow their existence to so cripple us that we are immobilized. There is a generation of children who simply cannot wait until other people change things for us.

In other words, no more excuses! It is high time for us to operate and draw from our strengths, rather than be duped into inertia due to a myth that is without substance or authority. It is time for the church to lead the way in replacing our culture's myopic thinking with long range, biblically-based strategies designed to aggressively reverse the state of affairs in urban America. We must join hands with others from different cultures who also realize their strengths under God and who are willing to accept ours and together change the state of affairs in our community (and their community as well).

In the words of a song by the Winans, "It's Time for a Change," and the time is now. If not you, who? If not now, when? The Bible stands as the only sufficient authority and source for providing the appropriate basis for racial pride, guidelines for successfully addressing racial issues, and glue for maintaining racial unity. Only by allowing the Bible, operating through committed Christians in both the Black and White church, to be the standard by which we judge ourselves and others, can we re-experience the power necessary to be the kind of salt and light that can save a decaying society.

SELECTED BIBLIOGRAPHY

Allen, Hank. "The Black Family: Its unique legacy, current challenges and future prospects." *The Black Family: Past, Present and Future*. Edited by Lee N. June. Grand Rapids: Zondervan Publishing House, 1991.

Bankole, Timothy. *Missionary Shepherds and African Sheep*. Ibadan: Daystar Press, 1971.

Banks, William L. *The Black Church in the U.S.* Chicago: Moody Press, 1972.

Bauer, Ardnt, Gingrich and Danker. *A Greek-English Lexicon of the New Testament and Other Early Christian Literature*. Chicago and London: University of Chicago Press, 1979.

Bennett, Lerone, Jr. *Before the Mayflower*. Chicago: Moody Press, 1982.

Bentley, William H. *National Black Evangelical Association*. Chicago: William H. Bentley, 1979.

Brink, William, and Harris, Lewis. *The Negro Revolution in America*. New York: Simon and Schuster, 1964.

Brown, Driver and Briggs. *A Hebrew English Lexicon of the Old Testament*. London: Oxford University Press, 1968.

Carter, Harold A. *The Prayer Tradition of Black People*. Valley Forge, Pa.: Judson Press, 1976.

Cleage, Albert B., Jr. *The Black Messiah*. New York: Dell Publishing Co., Inc., 1967.

Cone, James H. *A Black Theology of Liberation*. Philadelphia and New York: J. B. Lippincott Company, 1970.

_____. *God of the Oppressed*. New York: The Seabury Press, 1975.

_____. *The Spirituals and the Blues*. New York: Seabury Press, 1972.

Copher, Charles B. "The Black Presence in the Old Testament." *Stony the Road We Trod*. Edited by Cain Hope Felder. Minneapolis: Fortress Press, 1991. pp. 146-64.

Corinth. *The International Standard Bible Encyclopedia*, vol. 1. Grand Rapids: Eerdmans, 1979.

Dictionary of Christianity in America. Edited by Daniel G. Reid. Downers Grove, Ill.: InterVarsity Press, 1990.

DuBois, W. E. B. *The Souls of Black Folk.* New York: Fawcett Publications, Inc., 1953.

_____. *The Negro.* New York: Oxford University Press, 1970.

Elwell, Walter. *The Evangelical Theological Dictionary.* Grand Rapids: Baker Book House, 1989.

Evans, Anthony T. *Biblical Theology and the Black Experience.* Dallas: Black Evangelistic Enterprise, 1977.

_____. *Guiding Your Family in a Misguided World.* Pomona, Calif.: Focus on the Family, 1991.

Fee, Gordon. *The First Epistle to the Corinthians.* Grand Rapids: Eerdmans, 1987.

Felder, Cain Hope. *Troubling Biblical Waters: Race, Class, and Family.* Maryknoll, N.Y.: Orbis Books, 1989.

Frazier, E. Franklin. *The Negro Church in America.* Lincoln, C. Eric. *The Black Church Since Frazier.* New York: Schocken Books, 1963.

Frobenius, Leo. *The Voice of Africa.* London: Oxford University Press, 1913.

Goldston, Robert. *The Negro Revolution.* Toronto: The Macmillan Company, 1969.

Hamilton, Charles V. *The Black Preacher in America.* New York: William Morrow and Company, Inc., 1972.

Hamilton, Edith. *Mythology.* New York and Scarborough, Ontario: Mentor, 1969.

Harding, Vincent. *There Is a River.* New York: Harcourt Brace Jovanovich, Publishers, 1981.

Hicks, Jr., H. Beecher. *Images of the Black Preacher: The Man Nobody Knows.* Valley Forge, Pa.: Judson Press, 1977.

Hodge, A. A. *Outlines in Theology.* Carlisle, Pa.: Banner of Truth, 1972.

Idowu, E. Bolaji. *Olòdúmarè God in Yoruba Belief.* London: Longmans, 1962.

Keil, C. F. and Delitzsch, F. "The Pentateuch." In *Commentary on the Old Testament in Ten Volumes.* Vol. 10. Reprint (25 vols. in 10). Grand Rapids: William B. Eerdmans Publishing Company, 1978.

Kittel, Gerhard and Friedrick, Gerhard, eds. *Theological Dictionary of the New Testament.* Translated and edited by Geoffrey W. Bromiley. Volume II, Grand Rapids: Eerdmans, 1987.

Kunjufu, Jawanza. *Developing Positive Self-Images and Discipline in Black Children.* Chicago: African-American Images, 1984.

_____. *Countering the Conspiracy to Destroy Black Boys.* Vols. I and II, Chicago: African-American Images, 1985.

Liddell, Henry George and Scott, Robert. *Greek-English Lexicon.* Oxford: Oxford, 1989.

Lincoln, C. Eric. *The Black Experience in Religion.* Garden City, N.Y.: Anchor Books, 1974.

_____ and Mamiya, Lawrence H. *The Black Church in the African-American Experience.* Durham: Duke University Press, 1990.

Lovell, John, Jr. *Black Song: The Forge and the Flame.* New York: The Macmillan Company, 1972.

McCall, Emmanuel L. "Black and White Together." In *The Black Christian Experience.* Edited by Emmanuel L. McCall. Nashville: Broadman Press, 1972.

McCray, Walter Arthur. *The Black Presence in the Bible.* Chicago: Black Light Fellowship, 1990.

_____. *The Black Presence in the Bible and the Table of Nations.* Chicago: Black Light Fellowship, 1990.

McKissic, William Dwight, Jr. *Beyond Roots: In Search of Blacks in the Bible.* Wenonah, N.J.: Renaissance Productions, 1990.

Mitchell, Henry H. *Black Belief.* New York: Harper and Row, Publishers, 1975.

_____. *Black Preaching.* San Francisco: Harper and Row, Publishers, 1979.

_____. "Black Preaching." *The Black Christian Experience.* Compiled by Emmanuel L. McCall. Nashville, Tenn.: Broadman Press, 1972.

Olowola, C. "The Concept of Sacrifice in Yoruba Religion." DTS Thesis, 1976.

Paris, Peter J. *The Social Teaching of the Black Churches.* Philadelphia: Fortress Press, 1985.

Roberts, J. Deotis. *A Black Political Theology.* Philadelphia: The Westminster Press, 1974.

_____. *Liberation and Reconciliation: A Black Theology.* Philadelphia: The Westminster Press, 1952.

Ryrie, Charles Caldwell. *Biblical Theology of the New Testament.* Chicago: Moody Press, 1959.

_____. "Perspectives on Social Ethics--Part I: Theological Perspectives on Social Ethics." *Bibliotheca Sacra* 138 (Jan.-Mar. 1977): 33-44.

_____. *A Survey of Bible Doctrine.* Chicago: Moody Press, 1972.

Skinner, Tom. *How Black Is the Gospel.* Philadelphia and New York: J. B. Lippincott Company, 1970.

_____. *If Christ Is the Answer, What Are the Questions?* Grand Rapids: Zondervan Publishing House, 1974.

Steele, Shelby. *The Content of Our Character.* New York: St. Martin's Press, 1990.

Soulen, Richard N. "Black Worship and Hermeneutic." *Christian Century,* 87 (June 1970), pp. 169-70.

Sweet, William W. *The Story of Religion in America.* Grand Rapids: Baker Book House, 1973.

Wilmore, Gayraud S. *Black Religion and Black Radicalism.* Garden City, N.Y.: Anchor Press/Doubleday, 1973.

The Zondervan Pictoral Encyclopedia of the Bible. Edited by Merrell C. Tenney, 1975. S. v. "Gospel (Message)," by D. R. Jackson, 2:779-84; S. v. "Liberty," by W. H. Mare, 3:920-21; S. v. "Sanhedrin" D. A. Hagner, 5:268-73.